HIDDEN SECRETS

OF

INVESTING

CORRUPTION OF REAL MONEY (PART III)

FIRST EDITION

MARCO CHU KWAN CHING

BOOKS IN THE

CORRUPTION OF REAL MONEY SERIES
by Marco Chu Kwan Ching

CORRUPTION OF REAL MONEY

LEGACY OF DEBT

HIDDEN SECRETS OF INVESTING

WEALTH CYCLES IN GOLD AND SILVER

CONSPIRACY OF SHADOW BANK

AGE OF CRYPTOCURRENCY

EVERYTHING ON OIL & ENERGY

CRYSTAL BALLS OF THE 21ST CENTURY

HIDDEN SECRETS
OF INVESTING

FIRST EDITION

MARCO CHU KWAN CHING

This publication is designed to provide competent and reliable information regarding the subject matter covered. However, it is sold with the understanding that the author and publisher are not engaged in rendering legal, financial, or other professional advice. Laws and practices often vary from state to state and country to country, and if legal or other expert assistance is required, the service of a professional should be sought. The author and publisher specifically disclaim any liability incurred from the use or application from the content of this book. All investing activities involve risk. Any decision made in the financial market should be made after thorough research.

"To Mom and Dad"

Acknowledgements

Where do I begin thanking all the people who helped to make this book possible? This book represents one of my most dedicated missions of my life.

I would like to express my gratitude to my parents, Angela Tsang and Tony Chu, for their encouragement. I would like to give special thanks to Mike Maloney who started me on the road to invest in precious metals; Donald Trump for sharing his valuable expereince in real estate; Robert Kiyosaki for his wisdom in financial education and to Peter Schiff for his unparalleled economic insights; Ron Paul for his diligent politics lectures. I would like to thank Michele Berner for proofreading my book; I especially like to thank my grandparents, as my childhood with them is instrumental in bringing this book to fruition.

Contents

Introduction

Part I: Are You Prepared to be an Investor?

Chapter 1   Do you Plan to Work Hard Forever?................................1

Chapter 2   The Animal Inside Us..13

Chapter 3   Riddles of the Market...28

Part II: Before you Invest a Single Dollar

Chapter 4   The Concept of ROI...38

Chapter 5   S.M.A.R.T Goal..45

Chapter 6   Loopholes of the Rich..51

Chapter 7   Beware of the Naysayer Inside you.........................59

Part III: Hidden Secrets of Investing

Chapter 8   Hidden Secrets of Residential Real Estate.................67

Chapter 9   Hidden Secrets of Commercial Real Estate...............114

Chapter 10   Hidden Secrets of Property Development..................136

Chapter 11   Hidden Secrets of Stocks...148

Chapter 12   Hidden Secrets of Gold and Silver...........................190

Chapter 13   Hidden Secrets of Cryptocurrency............................203

Chapter 14   Hidden Secrets of Commodity..................................214

Chapter 15   Hidden Secrets of FOREX.......................................227

Chapter 16   Final Words...233

Introduction

Why did I write this book?

Does the world really need another book on investing? I struggled a lot before I began. Like the subject of money, the subject itself is complex, and there is no shortage of writers. Yet, many of this investing advice today is either outdated or impractical due to the change in the nature of the modern economy. Despite being logical, some of this advice can be dangerous if applied today. I wish to make a difference.

This book is the 3rd book in the *Corruption of Real Money* series. It is a journey on investing. The concepts that are presented in this book are based on the framework of my previous two books - *Corruption of Real Money* and *Legacy of Debt*, which talk about the subject of money, debt and the global economy. Personally, I strongly believe that understanding how the global economy works today is crucial if you want to be successful in investing. So, if you have read them, you will understand this book better.

There is an old saying that investing in what is comfortable is rarely profitable. Please expect the materials presented in this book to defy your comfort zone. Inside this book is years of valuable experience from highly successful investors around the world. Because the subject of investing is vast, it is normal that you may not be able to digest everything in this book in one go. But don't worry, like my previous books, this book is designed to be an easy read.

I hope the material I am about to present in this book will make you find investing interesting and exciting. More importantly, I hope you enjoy reading it. Now, turn to the next page, the hidden secrets await you.

What is Investing?

The legendary investor Warren Buffett defines investing as the process of laying out money now to receive more money in the future.

In other words, investing is about working smarter with your money, not harder for money.

The harder your money works for you, the less you need to work.

Your ultimate goal of investing is to have money continue to work for you even though you do not need to work physically.

Why Must You Invest?

In the past, investing was an option.

Today, it is crucial.

Casey Research has done research on the purchasing power of the U.S. dollar. What they found is that the value of our dollar has lost 95% of its value since 1913. This is not just in the U.S. but also around the world.

Figure 1: The Value of the U.S. dollar

Source: U.S. Bureau of Labor Statistics

The decline in the value of the dollar is the core reason why everything is getting so expensive today.

Inflation is not only a phenomenon.

Money is a plan to transfer your wealth away from you.

If you wonder why 1913 has been used as a reference point in Figure 1, I encourage you to read my first book *Corruption of Real Money* as I have described that plan in my book in depth.

The figure above is ringing an alarm bell to our future generation.

And that is why we must all be investors.

Money Rule

Believe it or not, if you do not have rules on money, the money will rule you.

Below are some main rules that you MUST follow religiously if you want to be a successful investor.

1.   You make money when you buy, not when you sell

2.   Invest your time wisely in finding or creating assets

3.   Learn to use OPM, OPT and OPR

4.   Be a master of debt

5.   Find a mentor

If these rules are puzzling you, don't worry. I will elaborate them in the rest of the book. Your ultimate goal is to understand these rules and apply them in your investment strategies.

[Note: An asset puts money into your pocket. OPM is defined as "Other People's Money." OPT is defined as "Other People's Time." OPR is defined as "Other People's Resources."]

The Importance of Financial Statement

At school, we receive a school report card to tell us about our grades.

When we have our health check, our doctors will present us with a report card to tell us about our health.

Before we invest, we need a financial statement to tell us our financial health.

A financial statement is like an X-ray of our financial health. It comprises an income statement and a balance sheet.

The feedback of the financial statement is very important as it tells you what is happening to you financially.

So, before you invest, I encourage you to form a habit of doing the following exercise every month.

Income

Income Type	Amount
Salary	$5,000
Business	$1,500
Real Estate	$300

Expense

Expense Type	Amount
Mortgage or Rent	$2000
Tax	$1000
Food & Clothing	$500
Utilities	$150
Transport	$120

Figure 2: Income Statement

Exercise 1: Creating an Income Statement

1.   Write down ALL the income sources you have and the amount in the INCOME BOX.

2.   Write down ALL the expenses you have and the amount in the EXPENSE BOX.

3.   Calculate the sum of the total assets.

4.   Calculate the sum of the total expenses.

5.   Calculate Net Cash Flow (Total Asset – Total Expense).

After you have done this exercise, you will have a Net Cash flow.

If you have a positive value, congratulations, you are financially healthy. You can proceed to Exercise 3.

If you have a negative value, I encourage you to do Exercise 2.

Exercise 2: Cutting Expenses

1.   Study your expense column carefully.

2.   List all the expenses that are unnecessary.

3.   Promise yourself not to incur those expenses the next month.

4.   Redo Exercise 1 again the following month. Repeat until you have a positive net saving.

After you have a positive saving, proceed to Exercise 3.

Exercise 3: Improving the Net Saving

1.   Study your asset column carefully.

2.   List 2 new ways to improve your current income and your target amount.

3.   Study your expense column carefully.

4.   List 2 new ways to cut your current expenses and your target amount.

5.   Calculate the sum of the total assets and total expenses again.

6.   Calculate the new Net Cash Flow (Total Asset – Total Expense).

The new cash flow is your target for next month.

If you have done the above exercises, congratulations, you have successfully developed your own income statement.

Next, we want to create your personal balance sheet.

A balance sheet contains two columns: Assets and Liabilites.

Assets pay you, and liabilities cost you.

Assets can be savings, stocks, real estate, bonds, gold, silver or business, etc.

Liabilities can be a mortgage, credit cards, car loans, etc.

Exercise 4: Creating a Balance Sheet

1.   Write down your current saving in the ASSET BOX.

2.   Write down ALL the assets you have and the amount in the ASSET BOX.

3.   Write down ALL the liabilities you have and the amount in the LIABILITY BOX.

If you have done the above exercises, congratulations, you have successfully developed your own balance sheet.

So, do you have a clearer picture of your financial standing now? Do you have positive cash flow? How many assets have you acquired?

Most likely, your situation will change with time.

So, it is very important that you form a habit and do this exercise every month.

Assets			Liabilities	
Assets Type		Amount	Liabilities Type	Amount
Stock (10 x AAPL @ $100/share)		$1,000	Home Mortgage	$600,000
Gold (10 ounce @ $1,600/ounce)		$16,000	School Loan	$70,000
			Credit Card	$200
Real Estate	Downpayment	Cost	Real Estate Mortgages	$400,000
Cow Street	$100,000	$500,000		

Figure 3: Balance Sheet

[Note: You can find a copy of the financial statement at the end of the book. Otherwise, you can download a soft copy at corruptionofrealmoney.com/financialstatement.php]

The Importance of Time Budgeting

Apart from your financial statement, time budgeting is also very important.

Time is the most valuable asset of all.

After all, everyone, whether you are rich or poor, only have 24 hours every day.

However, the way the rich spend their time is very, very different from the poor.

Tracking how you spent a week of your time and planning how you will spend your time from now on will drastically improve your financial situation.

So, I encourage you to do the following exercise:

1.   Record how you spent your time last week.

2.   Record how you will spend your time as an investor.

Exercise 5: Create a timesheet recording how you spent your time last week

Time Budget Grid							
Time	Sunday	Monday	Tuesday	Wednesday	Thursday	Friday	Saturday
12 a.m.							
1 a.m.							
2 a.m.							
3 a.m.							
4 a.m.							
5 a.m.							
6 a.m.							
7 a.m.							
8 a.m.							
9 a.m.							
10 a.m.							
11 a.m.							
12 p.m.							
1 p.m.							
2 p.m.							
3 p.m.							
4 p.m.							
5 p.m.							
6 p.m.							
7 p.m.							
8 p.m.							
9 p.m.							
10 p.m.							
11 p.m.							

Table 1: Time Budget

So, how many hours are you devoted to investing each day? How many hours are you watching TV? How many hours do you play video games or online shopping?

In the next exercise, I want you to put down how you will spend your time as an investor. This is the promise to yourself, and you should print this out and stick it on the wall next to your desk. It is important to see it every day.

Below are some examples of what an investor will do:

1. Analyzing investments
2. Reading investment books
3. Looking at real estate
4. Learning how to assemble deals
5. Learning how to evaluate deals
6. Studying the global economy
7. Learning how to start a business
8. Learning about OPM, OPT and OPR
9. Learning how to raise capital
10. Learning how to apply creative finance
11. Looking for opportunities
12. How to protect your investments using entities
13. How to reduce the amount of tax
14. How to use debt
15. How to invest with little or none of your own money
16. Increasing your financial IQ
17. Spending time with people with similar mindsets
18. Setting goals

Exercise 6: Create a time budget recording how much time you are dedicated to put into investing each week

Time Budget Grid							
Time	Sunday	Monday	Tuesday	Wednesday	Thursday	Friday	Saturday
12 a.m.							
1 a.m.							
2 a.m.							
3 a.m.							
4 a.m.							
5 a.m.							
6 a.m.							
7 a.m.							
8 a.m.							
9 a.m.							
10 a.m.							
11 a.m.							
12 p.m.							
1 p.m.							
2 p.m.							
3 p.m.							
4 p.m.							
5 p.m.							
6 p.m.							
7 p.m.							
8 p.m.							
9 p.m.							
10 p.m.							
11 p.m.							

Table 2: Time Budget

Your Goal of Saving

Your ultimate goal of investing is to have money continue to work for you even though you do not need to work physically.

To put this into perspective in your financial statement, it means:

$$\text{Total Income} - \text{Salary} > \text{Total Expense}$$

Why do I have to subtract the salary component?

It is because ultimately, you will retire, and you will not have a salary.

Your investment goal is to accumulate **income-producing assets** that can replace your salary.

Some of the traditional **income-producing assets** are real estate and stock dividends. However, there are *a lot more* different types of assets besides them.

Why should I be an Entrepreneur in the 21st Century?

I strongly believe that everyone should be an entrepreneur in the 21st century.

The Internet has created an unprecedented opportunity the world has ever seen. Technology has driven the cost and the risk of becoming an entrepreneur to zero.

To be successful in investing, one of the hidden secrets is to start a business.

But, how is investing and starting a business related? Why can't I just keep my daytime job and invest?

It may surprise you that there is a very, very big difference between investing through a business versus investing as an employee.

In fact, most people are rich because they do not invest as individuals but as business owners.

So, how does that work?

Cashflow Quadrant

Robert Kiyosaki, the author of *Rich Dad Poor Dad*, coined the term Cashflow Quadrant. It is the second book of Rich Dad series. This is a book that opened my eyes to the world of business and investing when I was twenty-years-old. I strongly recommend you get a copy.

The figure below is called the Cashflow Quadrant. Each of the quadrants has a letter.

The letter E stands for employee.

The letter S stands for self-employed.

The letter B stands for business owners.

The letter I stands for investor.

Figure 4: Cashflow Quadrant

Source: Rich Dad's Cashflow Quadrant

In each quadrant, there are different class of people with very different thinking and vocabulary about money. The people in each quadrant are governed by a very different set of tax laws.

An employee 'E' is anyone that works to earn a paycheck. An employee can be an accountant, an engineer, a waiter or even a manager. Their financial path is most likely to save money, buy a home, invest in the stock market and superannuation. To this group, **security** is their top priority. Their vocabularies are usually paycheck, pay rise, benefits and overtime. This group of people pays the second-highest in tax.

A self-employed 'S' is anyone who works for themselves. A self-employed can be a doctor, a dentist, a freelancer or a lawyer. To this group, **doing everything themselves** is their top priority. This group of people is smart people who specialize in what they do. Instead of working for someone, they own the job themselves. And if they do not work, their income stops. This group of people pays the highest in tax.

The letter '**B**' stands for big business - business, such as Facebook or Apple. Unlike the '**E**' and the '**S**', people operating in the '**B**' quadrant have a lot of tax benefits and pay as little as 20% in taxes. Instead of investing in the stock market, they create investments for others to invest in. They employ smart people on the left-hand side of the Cashflow Quadrant to work for them. In other words, they are leveraging OPM, OPT and OPR very effectively.

The letter '**I**' stands for investing. To operate successfully in the '**I**' quadrant, an investor is a master in using debt, business and real estate. A true investor effectively pays as little as **zero** in tax.

To put it into perspective, you will see that the left-hand side of the quadrant pays much higher taxes than the right-hand side of the quadrant.

Isn't this unfair?

Why is the tax law designed this way?

The truth is that there is a big reason for that.

Figure 5: Tax Payable in different Cashflow Quadrants
Source: Rich Dad's Cashflow Quadrant

Tax law is designed to encourage people to start a business and invest in real estate.

The tax law gives businesses a lot of incentives in tax so that it can provide employment to people. It gives incentives for people to invest in real estate to provide housing. People in the 'B' and 'I' quadrants are doing exactly what the government wants them to do, and that is why the government gives them tax breaks.

In fact, if you are operating in the '**I**' quadrant, the more money you make, the less tax you pay. The more debt you use, the less tax you pay. If you are investing in real estate strategically, the more real estate you accumulate, the less tax you pay. The bigger your business is, the less tax you pay.

Does it make sense to you?

Despite living in the same society, the mindsets of people in different quadrants are very different.

If you think about *working for money*, you will be paying a lot of taxes; if you *work for building assets*, you will pay a lot less in taxes.

Investing in the 21st Century

To be a successful investor in the 21st century, the number one skill you must learn is how to use debt.

If you revisit Figure 1 again, you will see the value of our dollar is going down because central banks around the world have been printing so much currency. By using good debt, you are essentially betting against the dollar. From 2008 until today, the Federal Reserve had increased the M2 money supply from $850 billion USD to over $3.5 trillion USD. The abundance of fiat currency has been driving down interest rates from all around the world.

The reason why the government creates so much money is to stimulate the economy.

A low interest rate means the government wants you to borrow and not save.

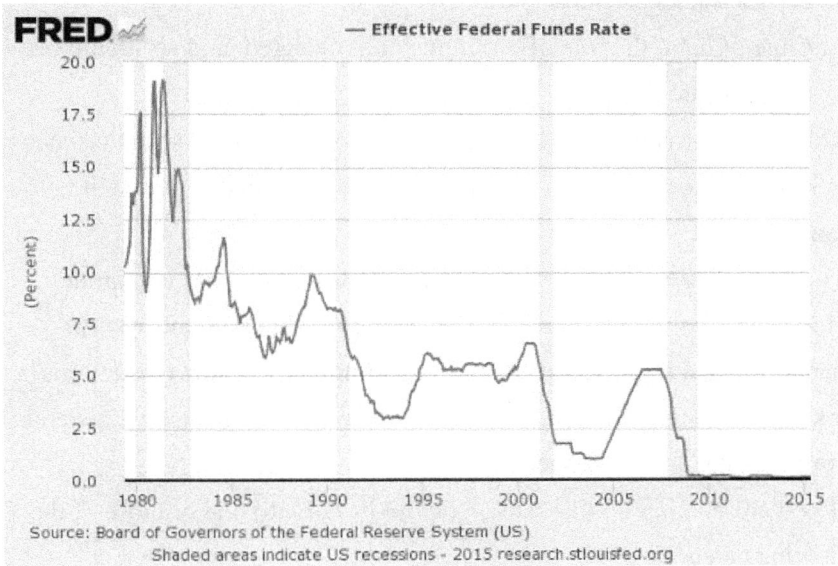

Figure 6: U.S. Interest Rate

Source: Federal Reserve

In the past, when money was pegged to gold, saving made sense.

In the 21st century, debt becomes the new money.

However, debt is a double-edged sword.

There are two types of debts – good debts and bad debts.

Good debts make you rich; bad debts make you poor.

Good debts are debts you incur to help you to create **income-produc-ing assets**; Bad debts are debts that reduce your income.

[Note: If you want to understand more about debts in the global economy today, I encourage you to get a copy of my book "*Legacy of Debt.*" You will appreciate the subject of debt a lot better.]

Who is this Book for?

In the age of debt, the rule of our money has changed, and so should our investment strategies.

This book is written for 21st century investors. It is a book that teaches you how to make money work harder for you. So one day, you will be financially free.

There is a famous investment quote: Only invest in what you know.

However, I do not think that just investing in what you know is sufficient. You will miss out on a lot of opportunities. For this reason, this book will cover a lot of investment classes so you can become a generalist in investing and not a specialist.

If you are picking up this book, you might fall into one or more of the following categories:

1.   People who are beginning to invest.

2.   People who love investing.

3.   People who are puzzled by investing.

4.   Investors with years of experience in investing.

5.   Investors who want to learn about the psychology of investing.

6.   Investors who want to explore different asset classes in investing.

7.   Investors who want to learn how to invest in real estate using little to none of your own money.

8.   Investors who want to learn how to use creative finance to invest in real estate.

9.   Investors who want to learn the hidden secrets in investing in stocks.

10.   Investors who want to learn the hidden secrets in investing in gold and silver.

11.   Investors who want to learn about cryptocurrency.

12.   Investors who want to learn the hidden secrets in commodity.

13.   Investors who want to learn about what drives the currency market today.

14.   People who want to criticize my book.

Part One: The first part of the book is about the mindset to be a successful investor. Chapter 1 will explore the basics of why you need to invest. Chapter 2 will talk about the psychology of investing. Chapter 3 will talk about the riddles of the market.

Part Two: The second part of the book is about what you should do before you invest a single dollar. Chapter 4 will explore the concept of ROI. Chapter 5 is about setting S.M.A.R.T goals. Chapter 6 is about how you can apply the same tax laws the rich do in investing. Chapter 7 is about training yourself to develop a healthy mindset in investing.

Part Three: The third part of the book is about investing techniques in each investment class. Chapter 8 is about the hidden secrets of residential real estate. You will learn about how to use creative finance to enter the real estate market, even without a job or deposit. Chapter 9 is about the hidden secrets of commercial real estate. You will learn about why commercial real estate is much better than residential real estate. I will guide you step by step on how to purchase commercial properties and how you can buy them below market value. Chapter 10 is about the hidden secrets of property development. You will learn the seven stages of property development and gain profit from it. By the end of these three chapters, I guarantee you will have a very deep knowledge about real estate investing that can be life-changing. Chapter 11 is about investing in stocks. In this chapter, I will show you the hidden secrets in stock investing to massively increase your chances of winning and decrease your chance of losing. I will also show you the technique Warren Buffett uses to position himself to profit whichever direction the market goes. Chapter 12 is about the hidden secrets of gold and silver. In this chapter, I will show you how to chart a definite path to true wealth using gold. You will also develop an instinct to identify if an asset is undervalued or overvalued. Chapter 13 is about how to invest in cryptocurrency. Chapter 14 is about investing in commodity. In this chapter, you will learn about the correlation between the commodity market and the stock market. By the end of this chapter, you will be confident about how to invest in commodity. Chapter 15 is about how to invest in FOREX. In the chapter, I will teach you what actually drives the currency market today.

This is a long journey in the subject of investing. I hope that by the end of the book, you will see the world of investing in a completely different way. Moreover, I hope this book is going to be a life-changing book for those who struggle to get ahead financially.

WELCOME TO THE HIDDEN SECRETS OF INVESTING

PART I

ARE YOU PREPARED TO BE AN INVESTOR?

Chapter 1

Do you Plan to Work Hard Forever?

"Risk comes from not knowing what you are doing"

-**Warren Buffett**

W hat do you want to do when you grow up?

This is probably the most important question we ask ourselves in our lifetime.

I am certain you have asked yourself this question at least once before.

This is a very important question because it decides where we are going in life.

When we were young, we dreamed about being an accountant, a police officer or an engineer. We then invested the first 20 years of our life in climbing the education ladder to meet that goal. Once we got there, we felt the excitement and joy. That's why you see graduates toss their graduation hats into the air, screaming at the top of their lungs. We did that because we are relieved from the education pressure and finally have the freedom we crave.

Do you have the same synergy?

By the time we got our dream job, most likely, we felt enthusiastic at the beginning.

1

As time passes, for most people, our enthusiasm will begin to decay.
An invisible pressure begins to surface - financial pressure.

I've encountered countless people who end up blaming their own dream job. They complain about how their income is disproportionate with the effort they put in. Finally, they feel discouraged and give in. "Have I chosen the wrong career path?"

Have I Chosen the Wrong Career Path?

It is natural to have this thought in the first place.

Believe it or not, you have not chosen the wrong career path.

Most career paths today will eventually lead to the same conclusion.

I have met countless people working in different fields. Whether they are dentists, accountants, engineers, storeowners or CEOs of big corporations, eventually, they all run into similar financial problems. They are constantly facing the situation of ever-increasing expenses with income not catching up.

In my opinion, none of us have chosen the wrong career; we have just chosen the wrong financial path.

We have a false perception that both paths equate.

In reality, they don't.

They are two very different paths.

A prosperous career path does not necessarily equate to a prosperous financial path.

What is Your Goal for Working?

I know people who work so hard and go nowhere in life. I also know people who work so little but enjoy a lot of freedom. Do you have a similar experience? Does this logic sound contradictory? What is your goal for working? More importantly, what are you working hard on?

To me, building a career and a financial path are both important.

After all, getting into the career path you desire is your dream from the beginning.

However, your career path will not chart a course for your financial freedom today. This is the reason why designing a financial path is crucial. I believe this is why you are seeking a possible alternative.

One of the reasons why I think people are struggling financially today is because they are mixing up the difference between a career path with their financial path. It is sad to see people spending their entire life working on perfecting their career path without even knowing a financial path exists.

Don't be one of them.

The Riskiest Thing in Life

My Grandad is a philosopher. He is my mentor in the subject of money. If you have read my first book *Corruption of Money*, you will remember that it was my grandad who introduced me to gold when I was eight. Besides that, he also taught me about the concept of investing, which is as crucial as the subject of money. One of the first lessons in investing I learnt is risk.

***

"Ching, what do you think pushed Christopher Columbus to embark on a voyage across the Atlantic?" Grandad asked.

"His adventurous spirit for exploration is a remarkable story of risk," I exclaimed.

"True. Before the late 15th century, people in exploration lived in the perception that the world was flat. So, for anyone setting off without knowing the accurate distance to their destination might mean death," Grandad said.

"No wonder why many people would rather believe the earth was flat than to set out for exploration," I concluded.

"To embark on his voyage, Columbus needed to raise a significant amount of funding. However, like all things in life, this was no smooth process. He had been rejected many times due to his calculations for the circumference of the globe. It took him seven years to raise the required funding to set out on his voyage across the Atlantic. He didn't get anywhere until he finally got credibility from his plans," Grandad continued.

"Seven years! Most people like me would have given up within seven days. What makes him so certain he could discover continents?" I exclaimed.

"It was his beliefs. It was his courage to take calculated risks. In fact, many of his sponsors did not believe he had such a significant find, and Columbus was offered extremely generous terms for his discovery. Terms like being appointed as the governor of any lands he discovered and given one-tenth of the revenues from those lands."

"The higher the risk taken, the higher the reward." I began to understand.

"What sets apart the successful and the unsuccessful is the mastery of risk. The return on calculated risk can sometimes, but not always, lead to spectacular success, glory and riches beyond the dreams of many people," Grandad spoke.

"Grandad, I guess you have taken a lot of calculated risks in the past," I guessed.

"I did. It was the most awful yet rewarding experience. Unlike your generation today, I was not living in times of peace. I was living in times of war. There were a lot of uncertainties due to the Japanese invasion in Hong Kong. The fear of communism and the confiscation of wealth caused a lot of people to flee this place. I took the risk to stay, as I believed British colonization would bring prosperity to this area. I predicted that this would be a tremendous opportunity in accumulating undervalued land, in businesses and international trade."

"But we are living in times of peace today. Even so, the middle classes are struggling every day to make a living. Many people are working hard just to make an ordinary life. I will be one of them," I sighed.

"I can tell," Grandad laughed. "Do you know the riskiest thing in life?"

"Not graduating from university," I responded.

"Well, you might think so at this stage in life. But reality is very different from school. The school system trains people to avoid taking risks; it is designed to punish people who make mistakes. Reality rewards risk-takers and punishes people who do not make enough mistakes. After all, risk and opportunities are both sides of the same coin," Grandad explained.

"Is that why so many 'A' students in school end up being a saver and live an ordinary life?" I added.

"That's correct. 'A' stands for academic, and 'C' stands for capitalists. It has nothing to do with their ability but their mindsets. If you are not willing to risk the unusual, you will have to settle with the ordinary. Avoiding risk is one of the riskiest things in life."

"Grandad, what do you suggest I do?"

"Start designing your own financial path."

Why Should you Design a Financial Path

"Unlike a career path where the university syllabus helps you to chart your course. A financial path is something you design," Grandad continued.

"A financial path?" I questioned.

"If you look around in the city, you see people, buildings and businesses, and each of them has a report card of their own. It is called a financial statement. A financial statement comprises two parts - an income statement and a balance sheet. Altogether, it tells the financial story of an entity, whether it is an asset or a person."

"I remember that you taught me a financial statement is like an X-Ray to diagnose financial health."

"Exactly." Grandad began a story as he drew me a diagram.

"Suppose John was an engineer, and his only income is his job. He is working for a big company with an annual salary package amount of 100,400 AUD, which is roughly 8,000 AUD per month. This is probably what most graduates dreamed of. Most people will call him rich just by looking at his income."

"I wish I could have such a salary package too..."

"But if you look at his expenses column, he has monthly expenses of 6,000 AUD per month to support his family. That gives him a net saving of 2,000 AUD per month."

"That is pretty satisfactory for me," I added.

"John felt satisfactory at the beginning too. A net saving of 2,000 AUD per month would ideally mean 24,000 AUD per year. In other words, if John is 25 years old, by the time he reaches the age of 65, he would have saved a little bit less than $1 million (i.e. 960,000 AUD). That was how he charted his financial path, and he felt happy." Grandad continued with the logic.

"But is $1 million enough to retire?" I hesitated as I recalled an article I'd read from Forbes –"*$1 Million In Retirement May Not Be Enough*"

"I am glad you're thinking about it in your early 20s. As John progressed into his mid-30s, he soon realized that something was wrong with his financial path. As his kids grew up, their education expenses increased. Inflation was causing all other expenses to increase too. He worried about the hike in interest rate as it increased the mortgage repayments. The expenses column was going up, but his income stayed the same. Instead of having a net saving of $2,000, now he merely breaks even."

"What did John do?" I questioned as I was listening.

"John blamed his boss for not giving him a pay rise after all these years he'd worked hard to contribute to the company."

"What did the boss do?" I pressured Grandad to continue his story.

"The boss fired him the next day," Grandad chuckled.

"Huh? What about John's original million dollar plan?" I felt shocked.

"The story is not over yet. Because John's career path is so specialized, he could not find another job that paid the same rate. After a long period of discouragement, he finally gave up and lowered his expectation. Instead of spending a moment to think about his financial path, he went back to university to study for another degree part-time. Eventually, he got a part-time job as a waiter, which paid far lower than his original job. He worked harder and harder for money every day but was going nowhere financially. He was stuck with high expenses, hoping things would turn around." Grandad continued.

I contemplated for a moment. This was exactly the path I was preparing myself. I was too ideal. I was definitely not preparing for the worst.

"Do you know why you should design your financial path? John's financial path is a typical financial path of a saver." Grandad tapped on my shoulder to wake me from my thoughts.

"Grandad, how should I design my financial path?" I asked.

How Should I design my Financial Path?

"I am glad you asked," Grandad replied. "Many people do not bother to ask themselves this question. Thinking is the hardest part to do in life, and that is why so few people engage in it. Instead of designing their own financial paths, many people leave their financial paths to be designed by other people like the government, the tax collectors, the banks and their boss at work."

"Grandad, you are right. How should I begin?" I questioned.

"First, you should begin by understanding the meaning of principles, facts and opinions," Grandad responded.

"Principles, facts and opinions?"

"Birth and death are principles. Sunrise and sunset are principles. When you let go of the apple in your hand, it falls onto the ground; this is a principle of physics. Principles do not change. They are governed by the law of nature."

"What about facts?" I asked curiously.

"Facts are something which really occur. When your parents told you that by going to school, getting a safe, secure job, working hard and saving money, you would have many things in life, this is a fact. This plan worked well for them. But a plan, which worked in past generations does not mean it will continue to work in future generations and beyond."

"But why is that?"

"Tax laws will change. Our economic fundamentals will change. The nature of our money will change. The way that the so-called *normal* older generations used to live is not the new *normal* your generation is facing today," Grandad explained.

"Using 1913 as a base point, our dollar has lost 95% of its value," I recalled Grandad's lessons on money.

"Good memory," Grandad smiled.

"What about opinions?" I asked.

"When someone tells you how difficult a maths problem is, how late a bus arrives, how beautiful a girl looks, how good a stock is, or how rich they are, these are all opinions. They are opinions because what they said are based on their beliefs and experience," Grandad explained.

"But many things are based on opinions," I protested.

"You are right. That's why you need to do your own research to verify these opinions. One of the reasons why I think people do poorly financially is because they do not know how to distinguish the difference between principles, facts and opinions. When a stockbroker says how good a stock performs, people will blindly follow. Rather than looking at the investment fundamental of that stock, they choose to listen to what they want to hear. Stockbrokers are just salesmen. They sell what their customers want to hear. If you don't do proper research, you are sold."

"I see. Grandad, but aren't you giving me opinions too?" I questioned.

"Yes. Everything you listen to is a form of opinion until you verify them yourself. You cannot design your financial path based on opinions."

"How about designing my financial path based on facts?" I called.

"You cannot do that either. Here is the catch. You need to **understand** what happened to the facts in the past and discover if they are facts in your generation. That means discovering what works in the past as well as in the future. In order to design your financial path, you need to understand wealth principles."

"Wealth principles?" I exclaimed.

The Harder Your Money Works, The Less You Work

"Ching, most people have only got one plan. This plan is to work hard forever. But the problem is that you only have 24 hours each day. You can only work so hard each day," Grandad continued.

"I remember you told me that. I remember you told me that instead of working harder and harder, learn to have money working for me instead," I recalled.

"Correct. This is wealth principle number one. Remember this. The harder your money works, the less you work."

"Is that why you keep a blind eye when I slack off?" I smiled.

"I didn't see anything," Grandad chuckled.

"Grandad, is that why you are not working? But...how can I make money work harder?" I began to sense the picture.

How do You Make Money Work Harder?

"If we revisit John's income statement, he has a net saving of 2,000 AUD every month, and he has been saving money for 1 year. This gives him a total saving of 24,000 AUD. Now, suppose he put all his savings in a bank called RipOff Bank, which pays 1% interest per year. By year's end, he would receive an interest payment of 240 AUD."

"That isn't much..." I said.

"Yes, you are right. In this case, John's money is working for him; it's just not working hard enough," Grandad spoke as he sipped a cup of tea.

"How can you measure how hard our money is working?" I asked.

"It is called the Return of Investment. (ROI)," Grandad explained as he scribbled on a piece of paper.

"What is ROI trying to tell us?" I asked curiously.

"When John put his money into RipOff Bank and collects the interest, this action is called investing. The ROI is like a gauge to measure how hard your money is working; in this case, 1%."

"The higher the ROI, the harder the money works, and the more money produced?" I added.

"Exactly. You can imagine your investment as a vehicle. Instead of taking you from one location to another, an investment vehicle transports you from one financial goal to another. "

"So putting money inside a bank may not a good idea today because this investment vehicle is too slow. But if this is the case, why are there so many people still putting their excess cash into the bank to collect interest?"

"This is because of risk. Different investment vehicles have different risks. An investment vehicle that offers high ROI is like a jet. If you learn how to fly it, it can take you to your financial destination within seconds. But if you do not know how to fly it, the end result can be catastrophic.

So that's why so many people would rather choose to ride an investment bike (i.e., putting money in a bank). After all, it is safe, and they feel comfortable."

"But Grandad, I want to learn how to ride a jet!" I exclaimed.

"Calm down," Grandad lowered his voice. "If you want to ride a jet, you must learn how to control yourself and be a good pilot. Finding an investment vehicle that offers high ROI is easy, the difficult part is control and discipline. You will learn more about it in your investment career. You can always find a Boeing 747 investment, but if you cannot control it, you will crash."

"Investing sounds so exciting all of a sudden. The harder money works, the less I will have to work. All I have to do is to shop for an investment with high ROI."

"You got the point," Grandad spoke.

How Do You Measure Wealth?

"Grandad, how do you retire financially free? Do you have a lot of money in your bank account?" I asked.

"No, I don't. I never have a lot of money in my bank account. In fact, I am technically broke."

"Huh? I don't understand. But I thought you are rich?" I was shocked.

"I am wealthy, not rich." Grandad smiled.

"What is the difference?" I asked suspiciously.

"If you have $1million in your bank account, then congratulations. You are a millionaire. You are rich, but you are not necessarily wealthy."

"But $1 million is a lot of money," I argued.

"It depends. It is not uncommon to hear news like $10 million lottery jackpot winner now lives from paycheck to paycheck. To be wealthy, you must first learn how to measure wealth."

"Suppose you have a saving of 5,000 AUD and a monthly expense of 1,000 AUD, your wealth is 5 months."

"Wealth is measured in time, not money," I responded.

Do you Plan to Work Hard Forever?

So what is your plan? Do you want to be rich or wealthy? Do you plan to work hard forever? Or would you rather plan to have your money working hard for you?

If you choose the latter option, then congratulations, you are on a definite path to true wealth and freedom.

If you have read my first book, *Corruption of Real Money*, you will probably know that the money (i.e., currency) we are using today is just a plan to transfer your wealth away from you. This is the main reason why you feel life is going backwards, the harder you work.

So, before you go deeper into this book, I would like to warn you that this book has a price. I do not mean the price you pay for this book. I am referring to the price of being a good investor. Being a good investor is not an overnight task. Investing is a process. It takes a lot of time and experience. During the process, you will face adversity. You will have up and down moments as markets do wear and scare people out.

But don't be afraid. The rest of the book will explain my case.

In order to migrate from the present to your financial goal, you need two things. First, you need to be a good investor, which is your mindset in investing. Second, you need to know how to find or create good investment vehicles, which are investment techniques. Lacking either one of these elements will not move you to your financial destination.

So, are you ready to become a good investor?

If you do, please turn to the next page.

Chapter 2

The Animal Inside Us

"I can calculate the movement of the stars, but not the madness of men."

-Sir Isaac Newton

"Sir Isaac Newton discovered the law of gravitation under an apple tree. The law of physics tells us that an apple eventually falls. It will not stay up on the apple tree forever. It is ironic how the great Newton discovered this principle of nature but failed to apply this to his investment portfolio. He lost almost all of his fortune in the Great South Sea Bubble," Grandad explained.

I listened as Grandad shared his wisdom in investing.

"Human beings are emotional. Even the most rational person can do something irrational when our animal inside us takes over. It is our nature. Markets are driven by greed and fear. It happens throughout the history of civilizations. Letting emotions take over rationality is the worst thing to do in investing. If you had experienced loss in some of the biggest crashes in the market, you'd probably learnt the lesson the tough way. The financial loss is bitter to swallow."

The Animal Spirit

"Ching, if you want to be a good investor, the first thing you must do is to understand two things - monetary history and investing psychology."

"Monetary history and investing psychology? They sound very different subjects to me," I felt puzzled.

"The reason why you need to understand monetary history is that history does repeat itself over time. It behaves in waves and cycles. If you can catch the waves by knowing which cycles you are in right now, you can make great gains in the long-term. But in the short-term, markets are driven more by investors' psychology."

"How does market psychology work?"

"The market is always and will always be driven by two things - Greed and Fear. This is our animal spirit. We are all greedy and fearful at some point. It is the wrestle of these two psychologies that cause markets to go up and down, boom and burst, doom and gloom," Grandad explained.

"Interesting. The market is nothing but a measurement of greed and fear. But how are greed and fear measured?"

Bull and Bear

"In the world of investing, greed is related to the impulse to buy, and fear is related to the impulse to sell. Greed is driven by the desire to make as much profit as possible, and fear is driven by the herd instinct to cut loss. These two emotions come into play in the bull and bear market," Grandad said as he touched his silver bull and bear statues on his desk. Every time I came into Grandad's room, these statues captured my vision.

"The bull and bear market?" I asked curiously.

"A bull represents an increase, and a bear represents a decrease. These terms are used because a bull thrusts its horns up into the air while a bear swipes its paws down."

"Everyone must love the bull market and hate the bear," I exclaimed.

"Not necessarily," Grandad smiled.

"What do you mean?" I asked suspiciously.

"Both the Bull and Bear market can help you to create a lot of wealth. You will learn more as your experience grows. Always remember to be friends with greed and fear. Ride with the trend. Be greedy when others are fearful. Be fearful when others are greedy."

"Is it that simple?" I sound surprised.

"It is easier said than done."

Markets Phases

Understanding different phases in the markets give you a huge advantage over the rest of the population that don't. Usually, during the panic stage, people are just reactionary to what happened. Even the smartest financial analysts on mainstream will only tell you that they did not see it coming because *this time is different.*

There are three phases to a bull market. Phase one is called the *Stealth Accumulation Phase*. Phase two is called the *Public Participation Phase*. The third phase is called the *Euphoria Phase* or *Mania Phase*.

STEALTH ACCUMULATION PHASE

This is the stage where most people do not realize a bull market has begun. This phase is at the bottom of the trough, where smart money gets into the market. Ironically, few have the stomach for it. There are two types of stealth accumulation phases. One is when the investment is silent from the mainstream. That is why it is called stealth. Another one is when it is actively reported by the mainstream. (i.e., the bear market.) If you manage to overcome your emotions, filter out the noise and enter the market at this phase, you are destined to reap great profit. There is the point where you *buy low, sell high.*

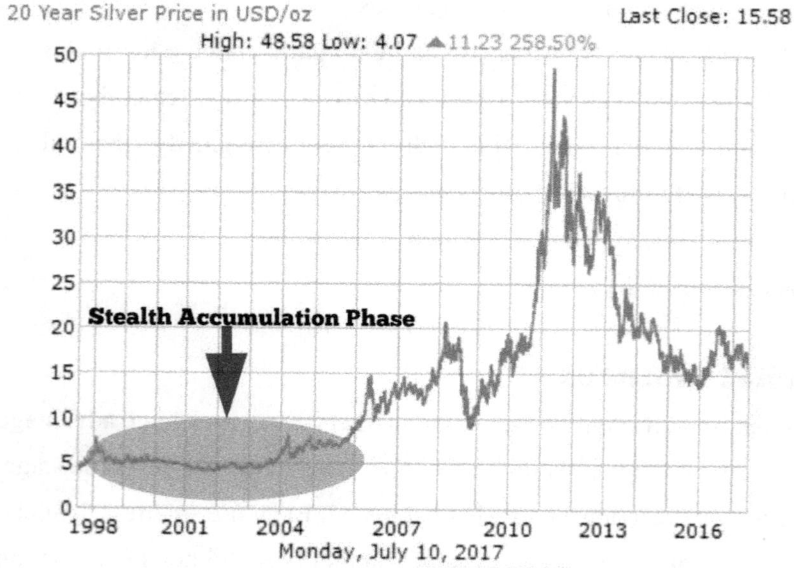
20 Year Silver Price in USD/oz
Last Close: 15.58
High: 48.58 Low: 4.07 ▲11.23 258.50%
50
45
40
35
30
25
20
15
10
5
0
Stealth Accumulation Phase
1998
2001
2004
2007
2010
2013
2016
Monday, July 10, 2017

Figure 2.1: Sealth Accumulatio Phase

Source: http://goldprice.org/

Is phase one of a bull market easy to recognize?

Obviously not. Sometimes, when an investment is in its bear market, it is hard to tell if it has reached rock bottom. Sometimes, an investment might only be at the second stage of further decline.

So are there no ways to spot whether we are in a stealth accumulation phase?

No. When the selling pressure starts to ease, and the downturn in price begins to level off, you will see prices bouncing up and down between a ceiling and a floor level. This is one of the signs that an investment might have reached a bottom.

PUBLIC PARTICIPATION PHASE

The public participation phase is the second phase of the bull market. It has the longest duration and the greatest gain. At this stage, people are aware of this investment. It hits the mainstream media. The public begins to realize it as it makes gain.

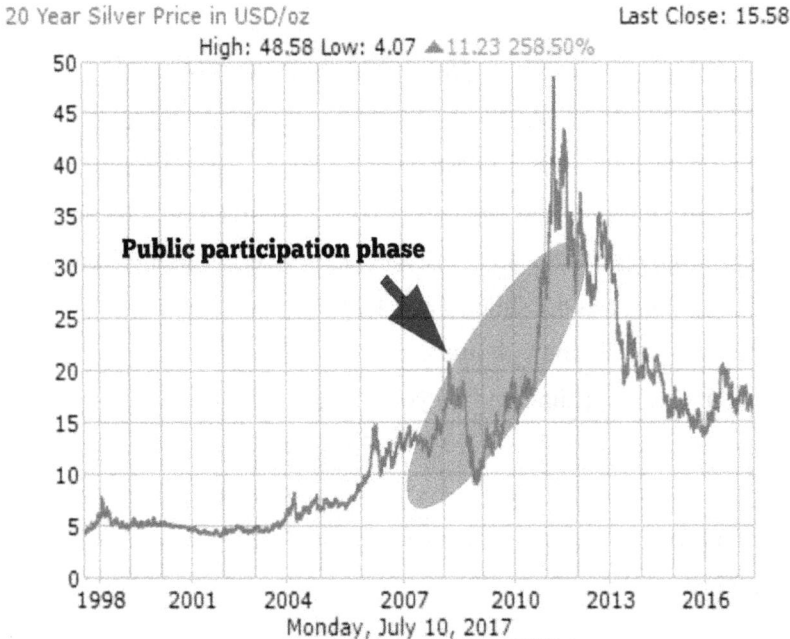

Figure 2.2: Public Participation Phase

Source: http://goldprice.org/

During this phase of the market, there are a lot of emotions involved. Optimism and scepticism drove the market. Without a solid fundamental understanding of your investment, you will be driven by the emotion of the market; in other words, the animal spirit.

Take silver as an example; when the price of silver moved from $8/oz in 2006 to a new high of $20/oz in 2008, there was a lot of optimism involved. Fundamental investors who entered the market at $4/oz in 2002 would have made five-fold their investment. But, at this point, would you enter the market? Is this a good point when there is too much optimism?

[Note: Unless you are a long-term fundamental investor who understands the true value of your investment, it is unwise to enter the market where the momentum is too optimistic.]

When the financial crisis hit in 2008, silver prices fell from $20/oz back to $8/oz, a 60% decline. During that period, the market suddenly turned from optimistic to pessimistic. Some investors bleed themselves to cut the loss; some hang onto their investment but are pessimistic that the price of silver might fall even further to $4/oz and stay there for a very long time. Back then, anything was possible. We just don't know unless by hindsight. So, the second phase of the bull market is also called the wall of worries.

But if you invest your time and do your own research, a wall of worries of an investment to others just means a pullback to you.

The second phase of a bull market is a rollercoaster ride. There will be a lot of ups and downs. These volatilities will shake out the weak such that the strong hands remain.

MANIA PHASE

When the bull market transits into the third phase, this is when the public finally wakes up and all charge into the market. The burst of the NASDAQ bubble in 2000 was a result of what happened. Companies see their stock price shoot up by simply adding a dot.com at the end of their company name. The public doesn't even care if the company is productive or not as they only want to grab a quick profit. This is the blow off when the public all went charging in. The funny part is that investors always chase yesterday's news. Those who are not financially educated are going to get slaughtered. When the dot.com bubble burst, a lot of wealth was vaporized. Infospace had its share peak at $1305/share in March 2000, and after the crash, it was down to $22/share.

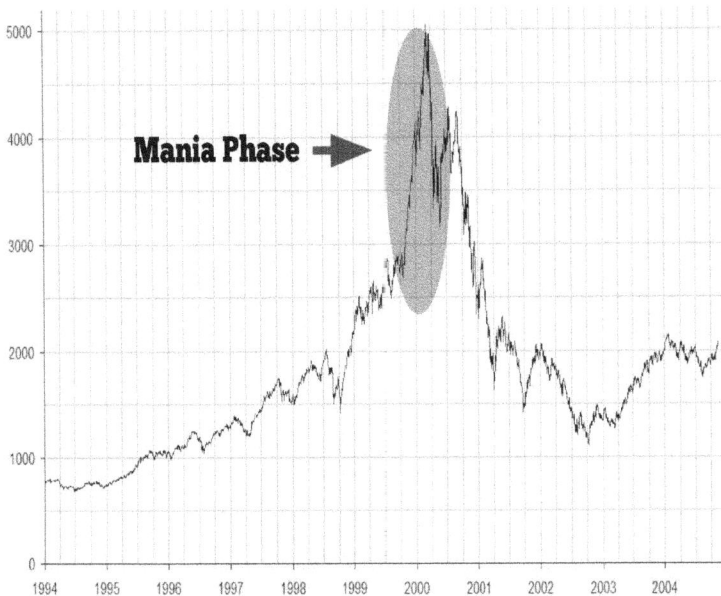

Figure 2.3: Mania Phase

Source:NASDAQ

The mania phase is usually very brief.

Those who were buying in the third phase might get a quick profit. But the sad reality is that the tide turns quicker than one can anticipate, and very few people realize it is time to get out. They hang onto their investment and hope for the market to rebound.

When the bull turns into a bear, there will be a short period of a paradigm shift, which is called a blow off phase. This happens like a hot knife through butter. During the blow off phase, there is a denial phase where people think the market must be overheated and needs to take a breath. But when the denial phase changes to fear, this is when you hear people saying, "THIS IS THE WORST POSSIBLE INVESTMENT I HAVE MADE IN MY LIFE!" This is exactly when you know that the bottom is near. This is when it is safe to accumulate again.

There is a saying that "If you hear a taxi driver ask you to get into the market because it is too good to be true, that's usually when you should get the hell out of the market as quickly as possible."

Madness of Crowds

"Men, it has been well said, think in herds; it will be seen that they go mad in herds, while they only recover their senses slowly, and one by one."

-CHARLES MACKAY, EXTRAORDINARY POPULAR DELUSIONS AND THE MADNESS OF CROWDS, 1841

"I am going to do an IQ test with you guys, but don't take this personally. On the left, you see a straight line labelled as 1. On the right, you see three lines of different lengths, labelled 2,3,4, respectively. Which line on the right has the same length as that on the left?"

Grandad was invited as a guest lecturer, and I was accompanying him in one of his classes. The theatre had a seating capacity of 300. There weren't many empty seats around. All students were highly-educated, and this was second year university.

Which Line has the same length as the line to the left?

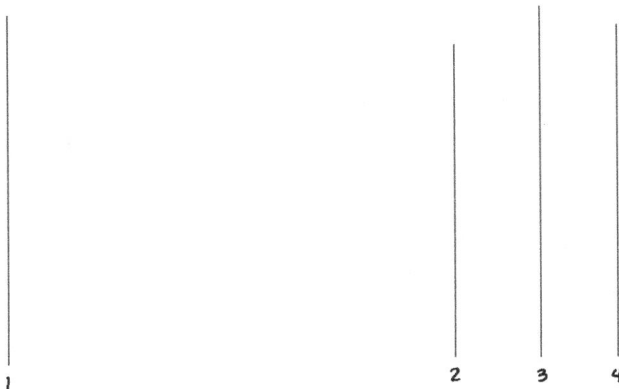

1   2   3   4

Figure 2.4: Compare length of line

Source:Author

"This is easy. Of course, it is number 3," I murmured without hesitation.

"If you think it is line 3, raise your hands," Grandad chuckled as he asked the class.

I was shocked as no one raised their hand. Could I be wrong? I felt uneasy.

"Now, if you think it is line 4, raise your hands."

Almost the whole class did apart from those sound sleepers at the back of the lecture theatre.

"Ching, your turn, what do you think?" Grandad asked me in front of the whole class.

"Ummm.....maybe line 4," I sounded nervous as I looked around.

"So, the final answer?" Grandad asked.

"Line 4," I assured.

"Well, this is a very important lesson to all of you who are about to learn how to invest," Grandad smiled.

Actually, the IQ test was a setup.

Grandad had deliberately instructed the whole class to give the wrong answer just to see what my response was. I was just the test subject of this experiment. I knew the answer, but I gave the wrong answer anyway that defied common sense in the end. This psychology is called herd mentality. In investing, it is called *groupthink*. People tend to herd like sheep because they value the wisdom of crowd behaviour over their common sense. If you have ever seen how herds move together upon danger, you will understand the logic behind it. Moving with the crowd always makes you feel safer than being unique.

The phenomenon of herding is, in fact, very real. Let me give you an example. If you are walking down a busy street, and you point to the sky, a tiny fraction of the pedestrians will stop and see what you are looking at. Most people will just walk by. But, if you gather ten people and point at the sky at the same time, you will find almost half of the pedestrians will stop even if the sky is empty. The more people looked at the sky, the higher the number of pedestrians will stop and find out what you are looking at. Interesting, isn't it. So how does this relate to investing?

Herding is part of the reason that causes the mania phase.

Investors base their judgment on unreasoning herd behaviour rather than common sense. They chase after yesterday's news, expecting there is always going to be the next fool who is going to pay more than them. In the mania phase, the buy and sell decisions are solely based on emotions rather than logic. The end result always ends in a blow off phase.

Are You Overconfident?

One morning, Grandad was reading a newspaper. The front page of the paper was titled *Horror nights on roads, a university student was badly injured last night after a car crash.*

"Grandad, I heard about it this morning. It was a tragic," I commented.

"Indeed. Ching, are you good at driving?" Grandad questioned.

"Well above average," I smiled.

"Eighty to ninety percent of college students will say they are a better and safer driver than the person next to them. Ironically, there are more accidents caused by college students," Grandad coughed.

"Why is that?" I wondered. My confidence sank.

"Overconfidence. Most young males are subjective. They exaggerate their own skills most of the time. They overestimate their knowledge and underestimate the role of chance."

I nodded. There is a lot of truth to that statement.

"There are many reasons why people become overconfident. In the context of investing, one of the reasons is hindsight. Hindsight falsely boosts a person's confidence level. By talking about something that happened in the past, a person talks like he had predicted this event in advance."

"Umm... I recall many financial advisors use hindsight to boost their creditability."

"Listening to financial advisors who talk hindsight can be very dangerous. Most of these financial advisors are actually salespeople. They are selling their hindsight to you to gain your trust and money. After all, they have their own KPI to meet. So, that is why investors must always do their own fundamental analysis on an investment. After all, past events do not always guarantee future events. History always repeats with a twist."

"But, why would people buy into financial advisors' hindsight?"

"Because people tend to be lazy. They prefer others to do research for them, so that's why they choose to listen to financial news. They prefer to listen to financial advisors' hindsight because it sounds logical and reasonable. Ironically, most explanations thrown out by mainstream financial analysts are not the real cause of the market movements. They are just opinions. In most cases, they do not know where the market will head."

"Now, I'm beginning to see why you encourage me to keep enriching my financial education," I began to absorb the lesson.

"Overconfidence leads to bias. Bias will close your door to open to new ideas and receive new information. That's why you should unlearn being overconfident. Always learn to be humble and not overconfident. Have a plan and be prepared for the plan to change."

The Art of Loss Aversion

"Grandad, do we have other animal behaviours within us?" I asked.

"There are plenty. Besides overconfidence, another one is called loss aversion," Grandad spoke as he ordered a cup of coffee.

"Loss aversion?" I sound curious.

Grandad took out a coin from his pocket. It was a Canadian Silver Maple Leaf. The coin was eye-catching. I wonder what lesson Grandad was trying to teach me.

"I am going to toss this coin, and if it's heads, you win $100. But, if it is tails, you lose $100. Fair deal, right?" Grandad offered as he teased me with the coin.

"Fair deal," I responded as Grandad began to flip his coin.

"Wait!" I hesitated suddenly.

"What is the matter?" Grandad asked.

"It is too risky..." I murmured.

"But it is a fair gamble," Grandad continued.

"I don't mean that it is not a fair gamble...I don't have enough money," I was trying to find an excuse.

"How about if the payout is $150?" Grandad continued.

I remained silent.

"How about $200?" Grandad gave me a wink.

"Ok, deal," I began to get motivated.

"Grandad, why don't you toss the coin?" I was impatient.

"It is a test. A test to find out about your loss aversion," Grandad smiled.

"My loss aversion?"

"Ching, why are you induced by $200 to take the bet?" Grandad asked.

"I don't know. Perhaps the bet sounds attractive," I frowned, not knowing where this conversation would lead.

"At first, you hesitated. Your pain of losing $100 is psychologically more powerful than your pleasure of gaining $100. Then, I changed the terms. That's why you accept this bet. It is a behaviour finance in which people are more likely to avoid losses than seek to gain something of equal value," Grandad explained. "But when I increase the gain, your risk aversion is lowered, and you accept the bet. In reality, everyone has different loss aversion levels. Normal people will take a bet when there is twice as much upside as there is downside. But, the interesting thing is that sometimes, when we face a situation where sure loss is involved, we are still overwhelmingly likely to take the gamble."

"How is that possible?" I was confused.

"The trick lies in how the bet or offer is framed," Grandad continues to explain. "Imagine you are the leader of a rescue mission on the September 11 attack, and you have to make either one of these decisions.

Decision A: 300 will be saved.

Decision B: 1/3 chance that 900 people will be saved. 2/3 chance that none will survive.

Ching, which decision would you make?"

"Of course, A," I answered.

"In both cases, both the expected value is 300. But people are risk-adverse in nature. It's not surprising that you would choose A over B. Now, here's the trick. How about if I reframed it as

Decision A: 300 will die.

Decision B: 1/3 chance that none will die. 2/3 chance that 450 people will survive.

What will you choose this time around?"

"Decision B."

"Ching, do you get my point? Even logic says both decisions have the same expected value. It is the framing of the decisions and your risk-seeking preferences that demonstrate which decision you will make. It happens every day for doctors as well as investors."

Behaviour Finance

This chapter is about behaviour finance. It is about how the psychological influence of investors can affect market outcomes. In reality, investors are not always rational; they have limits to their self-control and are influenced by their own biases.

The charts you see in the market actually describe investor behaviour. Over time, people discover these charts form certain patterns that repeat themselves. Some of these patterns are more recognizable than others. Analysing charts in the market is called technical analysis, which attributes to behavioural finance.

In reality, human psychology in the financial market has remained much the same ever since the stock market exists. Overconfidence, loss aversion, and herding are cognitive biases that will continue as long as the market exists. It is the animal inside us.

Chapter 3

Riddles of the Market

Financial experts like to use logic and reasons to rationalise how markets behave. Despite sound reasoning and years of experience, most of their forecasts are either wrong or never happen.

So, is the market truly unpredictable?

If not, how come legendary investors like Warren Buffett are able to defy the odds of the market?

This chapter is about the riddles of the market.

Before you continue, please be advised that the concepts in this chapter might be difficult to grasp in one go. What you are about to learn in this chapter is very different from traditional investing thinking. So I encourage you to revise this chapter later on to let the ideas sink in.

Are You Listening to Armatures or Experts?

After following the financial markets for years, one thing I find particularly interesting is that most financial experts and economists tend to fail miserably at their short-term predictions.

One of the common questions financial experts are asked in CNBC is the price target of an asset. As simple as the question may sound, it is one

28

of the most difficult ones to answer. Young financial analysts often fall into the trap of predicting a price target as well as giving a timeframe. Experienced experts, on the other hand, would know how to retreat from these types of questions. They respond conservatively or avoid them strategically by saying:

"I don't have a crystal ball. But if it goes down, I will buy more."
"Every pullback is a gift."

If you boil down these statements down to its essence, you will realize the wisdom between the lines.

Expert financial analysts are simply honest by telling you they do not know where the market is going in the short-term, but they know where the market is heading in the long-term.

How Market Works?

If you are trading in the stock market, knowing a little bit more ahead of others can give you tremendous benefits. Whether the news is good or bad, it doesn't matter. If you can jump in just five minutes before the price is changed, you make money. The dynamics of market responses have created an industry that demands the speed of information. In other words, it is the speed of information that has tremendous value.

I bet anyone who is interested in finance should know about Reuters. Reuters is an international news organization owned by Thomson Reuters. Before the invention of the telegraph, Thomas Reuters created a financial information service using carrier pigeons. Whenever there was new information available, Mr. Reuter would fly the pigeons that were bought from Paris with the new information tied to them. That was how Reuters' insiders were notified with the new information first. This arrangement enabled the insiders to have hours or even days to make a killing ahead of others. The famous Thomson Reuters Corporation is still in the industry today. But, of course, the brilliant pigeon financial service has been replaced by telegraphy, and now it has become the Internet.

When average investors invest, they tend to look at the news, the Internet or listen to their stockbrokers or financial experts. Then they think about it for a day or a week before putting their bet. This is a big mistake. Investors fail to realize that they cannot routinely expect to profit from the same information that's already out there. If you are to profit from the stock market, you need to come up with something that can enable "you" to get the new information faster than the public.

The phenomenon of how market price reflects all relevant information is called the efficiency market hypothesis (EMH). This term was coined by economist Eugene Fama back in 1970. What EMH tries to tell us is as soon as new information becomes available, the price of stocks or securities accurately reflects them in their price immediately, without bias. If EMH is true, there will be no undervalue or overvalue of stock price. Every stock you see is selling at fair market value. In a nutshell, investors are unlikely to outperform the market without assessing new information before anyone else. And seasoned financial analysts in the media are no better at picking profitable stocks than throwing darts.

A Random Walk Down Wall Street

If the stock market is really efficient, like EMH suggests, any changes in stock price from day to day are due **only** to news.

But, news is unpredictable.

Therefore, stock price must have to be a random walk through time.

The stock market will behave like a drunken man in Wall Street, right? A drunken man moves directionless. Each of his steps will be random. One minute, he could be at the lamp pole, the next minute, he could be somewhere else. His position is best described by the following equation that describes a random walk.

$$x_t = A + x_{t-1} + \epsilon_t \quad \text{where} \quad \epsilon = \text{noises}, A = \text{constant}$$

[Note: The term "Random walk" was coined by a statistician, Karl Pearson, when he was writing his scientific journal - Nature, in 1905.]

What is interesting about the formula of a random walk is that it can be applied to the path traced by molecules of gas, Brownian motions, the steps of a drunk man, and even the financial status of a gambler, and so on.

Fooled by Randomness

Below is the Real S&P Composite Stock Price index from 1870 to today.

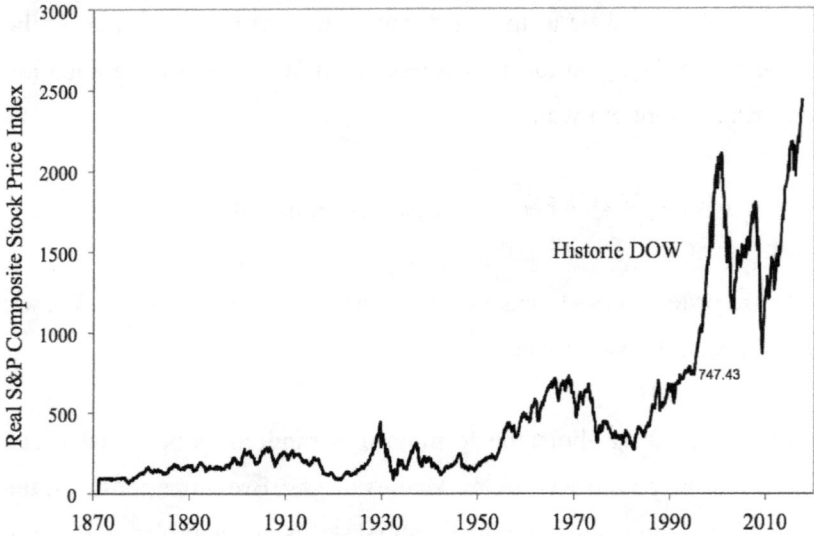

Figure 3.1: Real S&P Composite Stock Price Index

Source: http://www.econ.yale.edu/

If you apply the formula of a random walk onto Figure 3.2 in Excel and run several stimulations, you will arrive at random patterns.

Below is the first simulation I ran. The orange curve represents a random walk. And the black line is the historic DOW. Do you think they kind of look similar?

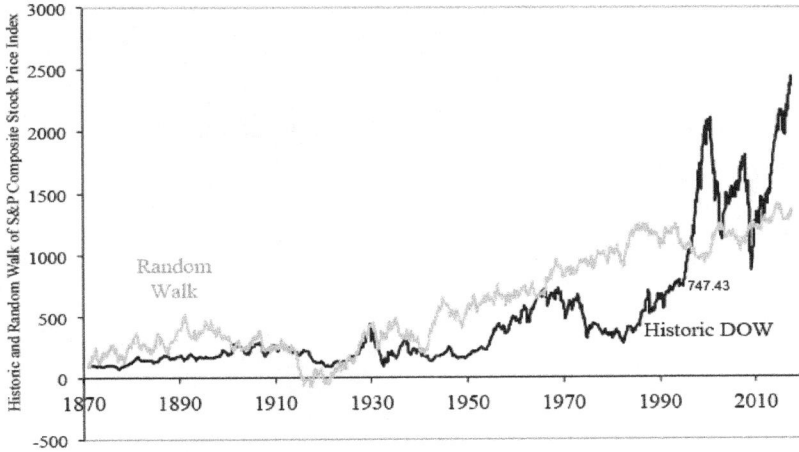

Figure 3.2: Stimulation 1

Source: Author

If you compare Figure 3.2 and Figure 3.3, without looking at the Random Walk label, both charts look like there are some kinds of patterns in them. Both of them have technical indicators as well as patterns.

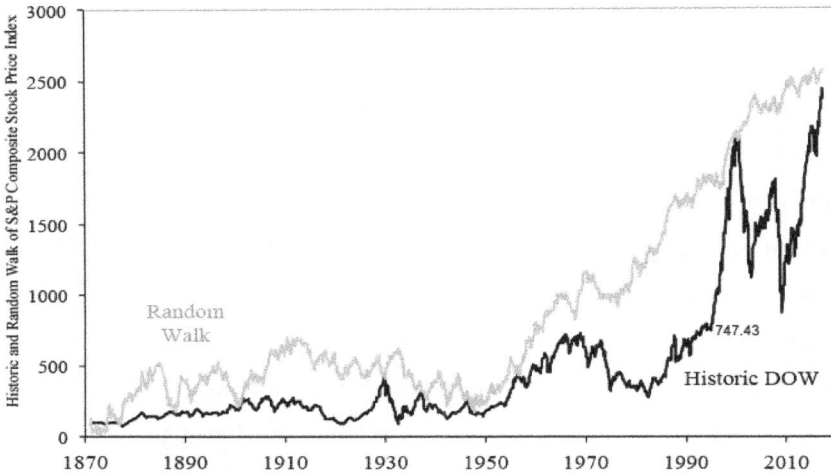

Figure 3.3: Stimulation 2 of Random Walk

Source: Author

People get deceived when they look at a stock price chart. They think they see patterns. So they try to come up with different theories to explain the charts.

If Figure 3.4 is the world we inherited today, what kind of economic models do you think economists will make out of it?

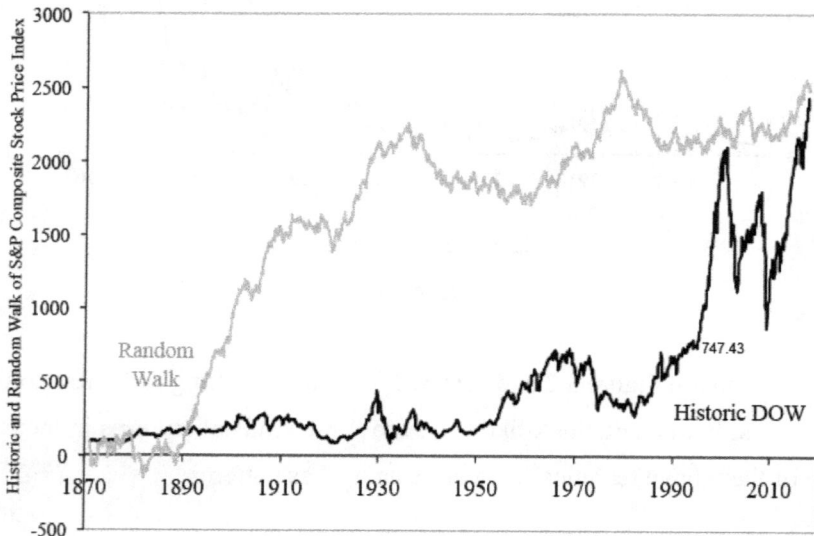

Figure 3.4: Stimulation 3 of Random Walk

Source: Author

The truth is that there are no patterns in these random walk charts. These charts are made up of points generated by the random walk equation only. That is why most of them, particularly Figure 3.3, look a lot like the actual stock market.

The insight from these simulations shows that there are actually no patterns in the stock market. All of the above simulations of the DOW can be our reality. Beating the market is not possible because it is driven by news, which is random and unpredictable. That is the main reason I think why financial gurus failed their prediction time after time. They are all fooled by the randomness of the market.

Riddles of the Market

Since the stock market exist, people have tried different ways to predict how the market works. Traders and speculators have tried to observe charts and patterns in the stock market to project future price movement, but they cannot win consistently.

This chapter has explained the concept of EMH and how the market moves randomly by news. It also proves that logic and reasons are not good tools to rationalize how markets behave, and why predicting the direction a market heads is actually a waste of time.

Before you invest a single dollar, I encourage you to turn to the next page and proceed to Part II.

PART II

BEFORE YOU INVEST A SINGLE DOLLAR

Chapter 4

The Concept of ROI

"Before you invest a single dollar, one of the most important things you must understand is the concept of ROI," Grandad said.

"What is ROI?" I asked curiously.

"ROI is the abbreviation of the Return of investment," Grandad said. "It is the most important number an investor primarily focuses on."

"How do I calculate ROI?" I pursued.

Grandad wrote the following formula on the whiteboard.

$$ROI = \frac{Profit}{Cost\ of\ Investment}$$

"Why is this formula important?" I questioned.

"It is because ROI tells you how experienced an investor is at investing," Grandad said. "For example, if you invest $1,000 in ABC stock and two years later, you sell it for $1,600, your ROI will be $600 / $1000 = 0.6 (60%).

"So, the ROI of an investment tells me how fast I will get my money back. The higher the ROI, the better the investment," I responded.

"Correct. Investors look at the ROI to quickly decide if an investment is worthwhile," Grandad responded.

"Interesting. How about calculating the ROI in real estate?" I responded.

$$ROI = \frac{Annual\ Profit}{Cost\ of\ Investment}$$

[Note: Profit = Annual rental income – Annual expense – Mortgage repayment.]

"Suppose you buy a $500,000 property with cash, and the closing cost is $20,000, bringing your total investment to $520,000 for the property. Suppose you collect $500 in rent every week. A year later, your rental income will be $26,000. Assume your expenses (strata, water and council) cost you $5,000 annually; your net annual rental income will become $21,000. To calculate your ROI, simply divide $21,000 by the $520,000. You will get a ROI of 4%.

"But not many people can afford to pay full price in cash," I murmured.

"Correct. Let's see what happens when you apply for a mortgage instead," Grandad explained.

"Could you please show me how it works?" I asked excitedly.

"Suppose this time, you bought the same $500,000 rental property, but instead of paying cash, you took out a mortgage. The down payment you need is 20% of the property price, which is $100,000. The closing cost is the same $20,000 as before, bringing you an out of pocket expense of $120,000. Let's say your mortgage is a 30-year loan with a fixed interest rate of 1.98%, your weekly principal and interest payment would be $340, or $17,680 annually. Assume your expenses (strata, water and council) cost you $5,000 annually, and your annual rental income is $500 per week or $26,000 per year. You annual cash flow will be $3,320 ($26,000 - $17,680 - $5000). In this case, your ROI will be 2.76%.

Investment Property

Total Price   : $500,000
Down payment : $100,000
Mortgage   : $400,000
(1.98 % p.a. ; 30 years fixed; Principal and interest.)

Annual Cashflow: $3,320
(Cash flow is rental income minus all expenses and mortgage repayment
Rental Income   = $26,000 per year.
Other Expense   = $5,000 per year
Mortgage Repayment   = $17,680 per year)

How to Improve the ROI?

"Ching, an ROI of 2.76% is pretty low. So, as an investor, how would you improve the ROI?" Grandad asked.

I paused for a while.

"Apart from raising the rent, I couldn't think of any other way," I shrugged.

"Very good, one way to increase the ROI is to increase the rent. But there might be other ways as well," Grandad replied.

"Are there really other ways?" I was curious.

"If you examine the mortgage closely, what can you see?" Grandad asked.

"Well, I see 1.98 % p.a.; 30 years fixed; Principal and interest. But, aren't these terms fixed?" I said.

"I am glad you asked. It is very important to develop the habit of asking. You may be surprised how much you can save just by asking in investing. A small variation in these numbers means a lot of difference to your investment. Imagine if you can manage to extend your 30 years mortgage to 35 years? What will happen to your ROI?"

"Umm..." I tried to think.

"You will reduce your monthly repayment by extending your loan term," Grandad smiled.

"That's interesting, but is that possible?" I said.

"Banks don't usually allow you to extend the repayment beyond 30 years. But, the younger you are, the higher the chance you will receive a 35-year loan. It never hurts to ask," Grandad replied.

"Can I ask the bank to lower the 1.98% interest rate too?" I speculated.

"You definitely should. Do not take what is written as the final rate you will receive. Instead, you should shop at different lenders for a rate that best fits you. Even half a percent down in interest rate may mean a lot to your ROI," Grandad advised.

"I see. What about the principal and interest component? Can I adjust that too?" I asked.

"Good question. You certainly can. There are two types of loans. The first type of loan is the **principal and interest**. This is the loan that you intend to pay off the mortgage. The second one is called an **interest only loan**, meaning you never intend to pay off the mortgage, but you pay the interest component only," Granddad explained.

"I remember what you taught me about the banks before. The banks never want us to pay down loans. The more loans, the better. All the banks care about is the interest they receive from the loan. Perhaps that is the primary reason why banks have loan package like interest only loan," I said.

"Good memory. But an interest only loan may only last for the first five years for some countries. Once the interest only period ends, you will start paying off the principal and interest. But, during the interest only period, interest only loans are one way to boost the ROI of your investment significantly," Grandad replied.

"That sounds like a good deal," I exclaimed.

"Ching, I hope you can see that a lot of the times, the ROI does not only depend on the investment but the investor. Now, look at this house. Assume our ROI is only 2.76%, do you think you can still improve it?" Grandad challenged.

"Well, can we improve the inside of the property?" I asked.

"Yes. And there are many ways to do it. You can furnish the space. You can add an extra bedroom. You can put a car space or storage space as well. In some cases, you can boost the cash flow by as much as $200 just by fitting out the property with simple, stylish pieces of furniture. That will boost your final ROI!" Grandad said.

"Wow. That's quite impressive," I was amused.

"The point is, that as an investor, you must think about ways to improve the ROI of your investment. Be an active investor. Work on how to reduce your expenses. Work on how to improve your rental income. You may be surprised at how much difference it can make in the long run," Grandad advised.

[Note: The above example is to describe how you can improve the ROI of your investment. You must do your own due diligence about various loans. Interest only loan has its pros and cons, which are subject to changes in the economy.]

ROI is Seen With Your Due Diligence, Not your Eyes

One day, I accompanied Grandad to inspect one of the properties he'd just accumulated in his portfolio.

At first, I thought it was going to be a nice, spacious property with sensational views.

Yet, by the time I arrived, it was nothing like I expected at all. The property was worn. The windows were old. The door creaked open when we entered inside. I definitely don't want to live there.

"Grandad, I think you might have bought a lemon this time," I said.

"Why do you say so?" Grandad asked curiously.

"Well, look at how old this place is. It looks like a haunted house. If this is a good investment, I bet pigs will fly," I looked around.

"ROI is seen with your due diligence, not your eyes," Grandad smiled.

"Due diligence?" I frowned.

Grandad and I walked over to an old window and looked outside.

"Did you see that train station over there?" Grandad pointed to a construction site.

"Yes. It is under construction. It will be very noisy. What has that got to do with your property?" I asked.

"Everything," Grandad assured.

"Everything?" I frowned.

"Perhaps it is time for you to learn to look at the property through the eye of an investor. A train station means convenience for transport. People love convenience. This train station will cause all the surrounding properties in this area to go up in value," Grandad said.

"But why do you risk buying this old unit? Why don't you buy a new one instead?" I asked.

"A new one in this area will cost $750,000, but an old one costs about $600,000. I bought this one because I can see the potential in this property. It would cost a lot less for me to repaint everything, knock down the windows and doors, and put new ones in. After the renovation, I can ask for the same rent as the $750,000 in this area," Grandad explained. "I can change the interior of the real estate, but I cannot change its location. That is why, instead of focusing on the interior of the property, you should do your due diligence about your location."

"What do you mean by due diligence about your location?" I scratched my head.

"It means finding out if the location is convenient for people to go to work. Look for developments like the train station or shopping centre further development that will boost the value of your property. Do research on your neighbourhoods. Find out if the property is a school catchment area. All these are part of your homework when you are going to invest in real estate. It is called due diligence."

Chapter 5

S.M.A.R.T Goals

"Many people fail in life, not for lack of ability or brains or even courage, but simply because they have never organised their energies around a goal."

-Elbert Hubbard

"So, Ching, are you sure you are ready to invest?" Grandad asked.

"Definitely!" I exclaimed.

"Congratulations. So, what is your plan?" Grandad asked.

"I want to buy many, many properties," I sounded excited.

"That is not good enough," Grandad shook his head.

"But, isn't property the way to true wealth? What is wrong with my plan?" I wondered.

"What you just said is not a goal. It is a wish," Grandad corrected me.

"A wish?" I was insulted.

"Many people just jump into investing without having any kind of direction where they want to be. Some set goals, but they often fail to achieve them. Perhaps it is time for you to be different from them. Perhaps it is time for you to make sure your goals are S.M.A.R.T," Grandad said.

Make your Goal S.M.A.R.T

The night, I learnt about S.M.A.R.T goals.

When we set benchmarks for things that we want to do, then we can achieve them. Without goals, we lose our sense of direction in what we want to do. This is not just for investing but everything in life as well.

However, just setting any goal is not good enough.

It is important to make sure your goals are S.M.A.R.T.

Every S.M.A.R.T goal must have five elements.

1.   Specific
2.   Measurable
3.   Attainable/ Accountable
4.   Realistic
5.   Timeline

Specific

A goal needs to be very specific. It needs to answer the six 'W' questions.

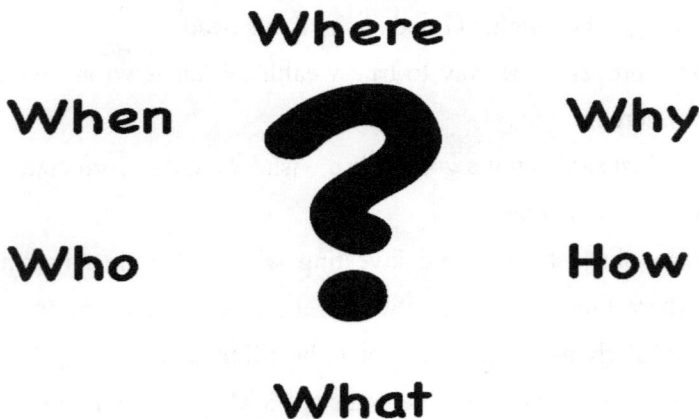

Where

When   **?**   **Why**

Who   **How**

What

Figure 5.1 Questions to ask yourself when investing

Source: Author

Some typical specific questions you should ask yourself in investing are:

- Where will I invest in?
- When will it be done by?
- How am I going to raise the capital?
- What specifically needs to be done?
- Who am I investing with?
- Why is this goal important to my investment plan?

Measurable

A goal needs to be measurable.

It is important to be measurable so that you will know what your progress is like and when you've achieved your goals.

Measurable is more about numbers. (e.g., "how many?" or "how much?" etc.)

Some typical specific questions you should ask yourself in investing are:

- How many ounces of gold am I going to buy?
- When will I buy them?

Attainable

A goal needs to be attainable.

As the investor, you should constantly ask yourself whether you are really committed to your investment goal.

For example, if your goal is $100 a month, it will not be attainable if you only have $50 left in your bank account after all the bills.

If your goal is not attainable, you are setting yourself up for failure.

Realistic

A goal needs to be small enough to achieve, but big enough to matter.

Above all, it needs to be realistic.

If you believe the goal is too hard or too easy, it probably is.

But you can always scale back or break it down into more manageable goals.

For example, "never drink coffee again" might be a lot more difficult than "only drink coffee once a week."

The ultimate idea of a realistic goal is that it should be challenging yet achievable.

Timeline

A goal needs to have a timeline.

Without a timeline, a goal is just a wish.

Without a sense of urgency, desires lose value.

A good timeline goal statement will be: When will I achieve my goal?

Weak Goals vs Strong Goals

Below are some examples of the difference between weak goals and strong goals.

Example 1

Weak Goals

I will buy many, many properties.

Strong Goals

I will accumulate one property in Hurstville that can generate $100 positive cashflow per month by year's end.

Example 2

Weak Goals

I will invest in gold bullion.

Strong Goals

I will accumulate one gold bullion coin by 31st July.

Goal to Financial Freedom

When you pick up this book, I guess your ultimate goal is to explore possible ways to achieve financial freedom. As I have promised you, this book will help you to chart your financial path to true wealth. But, in the end, everyone's path will be different. They are different because different readers have different circumstances that change with time.

Below is a FINANCIAL FREEDOM PLAN. It is a contract between you today and you in the future. It is your commitment to your future self.

For example:

Mr. X's Financial Freedom Plan

By 2030, I want to be financially free and have $70,000 a month in passive income.

My vision is to become a commercial real estate investor, so I can provide a better education for my children and spend more time with my family. Within five years, I wish to generate $100,000 in passive income to fund my retirement.

I want to invest in different types of commercial properties and achieve an average return of 20% so that I can retire with $10 million by 2040.

FINANCIAL FREEDOM PLAN

Your financial freedom plan provides direction, purposes and context for your investment. It provides the "why" behind the "what" and helps you to focus on your goals.

Vision About Your Future:_____

This is a clear metal picture of your financially independent future.

S.M.A.R.T Goals: _____

These are measurable objectives.

My Strategies: _____

These are the specific approaches to achieving the goals.

It may take you some time to sit and plan realistically.

Once you have written it, stick it on your desk, or anywhere that you can look at it every day.

It is a simple but very powerful way to keep you on track.

When I was writing this book, I also used this method to set goals. If I didn't, this book you are reading now would have probably never seen the light of day because life always gets in our way.

Please be advised that your goal will change along with time.

So, before you invest a single dollar and learn about the techniques in Part III, I strongly encourage you to do this exercise first to set your smart goals.

Chapter 6

Loopholes of the Rich

In any economy, the government wants you to do two primary things: create jobs and provide housing. The government does not actually want you to get a 9-5 job, doing overtime (OT), get a pay rise or bonuses. That's why your bonuses or overtime are taxed before even hitting your bank account? It is certainly a bitter experience.

But aren't we seeing the government focus on employment all the time in the news?

The government certainly does.

In fact, employment is the government's primary focus.

Unfortunately, the tax laws designed by the government do not favour employees and self-employed. They are written to reward entrepreneurs and real estate investors instead. If you do what the government wants you to do based on the tax laws, you can potentially reduce your tax significantly. If you don't, you will end up working harder as employees and self-employed, paying more tax.

Why do Investors and Business Owners Get Tax Breaks?

Unlike what most people think, the book on tax laws is nothing but a list of incentives for real estate investors and entrepreneurs.

The government understands that it is impossible for it to provide all jobs and housing in the economy. It is cheaper for the private sector to take care of these and provide incentives to them. For this reason, the government writes in the tax laws to allow entrepreneurs and investors to get all the tax benefits.

By understanding this simple logic, you will find that tax laws are not that scary at all. In this chapter, I am going to share with you how you might position yourself to use tax laws to your advantage in investing.

The Magic of Depreciation

Whether it is investing or starting a business, the first magic tax break that you must learn is called *depreciation*. Over time, an income-producing asset wears and tears. Its value declines over its lifespan. So, that is why the government allows you to claim tax deductions for the depreciation of your property. If the asset is tangible, like a property, it is called depreciation. On the other hand, if it an intangible asset, like the software you use in your business, it is called *amortization*. Either way, they have the same benefit.

The depreciation I particularly want to talk about here is regarding property. Anyone who purchases a property for income-producing purposes is entitled to depreciate the building and the content within it against their assessable income. Depreciation starts as soon as the property is placed in service or available to use as a rental. Most residential rental property is depreciated at a rate of 3.6% each year for 27.5 years. Let me give you an example.

[Note: The price of a property is divided into the three parts: the value of the building, its building content component and land. The land component cannot be depreciated, only the building and its contents can.]

Let's say, Mike brought a 2-bedroom apartment for $800,000. The land value is $200,000, and the value of the building and its contents is $600,000. Mike's depreciation on his property will look like this:

Mike's Depreciation on Investing Property	
Cost of 2-bedroom apartment	$800,000
Land Value	$200,000
Value of building and contents	$600,000
Depreciation of the Building	
Value of building and contents	$600,000
Value of building content	$100,000
Value of building	$500,000
Multiple the value of the building by the depreciation rate on the residential property	3.6%
Building Depreciation Deduction	$18,000
Depreciation of Building Content	
Value of building content	$100,000
Multiple by 20%	20%
Content Depreciation Deduction	$20,000
Total Depreciation of Building and Building Contents	
Building Depreciation Deduction	$18,000
Content Depreciation Deduction	$20,000
Total Depreciation	$38,000

Assume Mike's real estate income is $12,000. If he subtracts the depreciating expense of $38,000, he will get a loss of $26,000. Because the taxman is seeing a loss, Mike's entire $12,000 rental income is **tax-free**.

[Note: This example is based on the depreciation rule in the U.S. at the time of writing. Please check with your local accountant regarding depreciation rules as they vary from country to country.]

Tax Consequence	
Cash flow from Real Estate	$12,000
Minus total Depreciation	$38,000
Loss	($26,000)

In addition, Mike can use the $26,000 loss to offset against his other income. If Mike's income tax bracket is 40%, he will have the following tax consequences:

Potential Tax Refund	
Amount of loss that can be offset against other income	$26,000
Tax Bracket	$38,000
Potential tax refund	$10,400

[Note: In come countries, like Australia, this $10,400 is used to lower your tax bracket instead. Either way, it lowers the tax you pay.]

In a nutshell, the government is paying you to invest in real estate.

Depreciation is a magic to shelter a positive cashflow property from income tax by making it looks like it is losing money. Please remember to use it.

Earn Better Income

In 2019, an Australian millionaire earns more than $1 million in income a year. Yet, when it comes to tax time, his taxable income is under $18,000, meaning he paid no income tax.

Resident tax rates 2019–20

Taxable income	Tax on this income
0 – $18,200	Nil
$18,201 – $37,000	19c for each $1 over $18,200
$37,001 – $90,000	$3,572 plus 32.5c for each $1 over $37,000
$90,001 – $180,000	$20,797 plus 37c for each $1 over $90,000
$180,001 and over	$54,097 plus 45c for each $1 over $180,000

Figure 6.1: Australia Income Tax Bracket

Source: ATO

Like many other western countries, Australia has five income tax brackets. As you earn more than the thresholds of each bracket, you will be taxed at a higher rate. Say, if you earn an income of $90,000, and you are eligible to claim a business expense of $2,000 business deduction, this will move you one tax bracket lower. But to move down a tax bracket close to paying no income tax, you need financial IQ.

To begin, you need to pay attention to what type of income you are earning.

Every country has different types of income, mainly:

1.   Earned Income (e.g., Salary)
2.   Investment Income (e.g., capital gain from investment)
3.   Passive Income (e.g., real estate rental income)

Knowing these categories of income is very important as there are different tax laws attached to different types of income.

The first type of income is earned income. This income is taxed the highest. If you look at the Australian Income Tax Bracket, you will notice that the more you earn, the more you get taxed. At the highest income tax bracket, you are paying more than 45% of what you earn to the government.

Figure 6.2: Cashflow Quadrant
Source: Rich Dad's Cashflow Quadrant

The second type of income is investment income, which is divided into capital gain, interest and dividends. Capital gain is the income derived from buying and selling shares, ETF, options, futures, real estate, precious metal, cryptocurrencies, etc. Buy low and sell high incurs a tax called the capital gain tax (CGT). For instance, in Australia, when you make a capital gain, it is added to your assessable income and may significantly increase the tax you need to pay. CGT is calculated as part of your income tax, not a separate tax. Unfortunately, capital gain is where most people would invest their earned income in.

Dividend income is a different type of income, and a different set of tax law applies to it. If you buy shares that produce dividends, you may be able to claim a deduction for certain expenditure you incurred in deriving your income from those shares. This deductible includes management fees, interest and borrowing expenses (if you borrow money to buy dividends producing shares), travel expenses (travel costs to service your investment portfolio), and even the cost to subscribe to investment journals and publications. Apart from that, in Australia, some dividends incomes can be exempt from tax because of *franking credits*. Franked dividends have a franking credit attached to them, which represents the amount of tax the company has already paid. You are entitled to receive a credit for any tax the company has paid. If your top tax rate is less than the company's tax rate, the Australian Tax Office (ATO) will refund you the difference. However, in countries like the U.S., whether your dividend income is taxable depends on whether that dividend income you are receiving is qualified or not. Interest income, on the other hand, is mostly taxable. The interest amount will be added to your taxable income, and tax will be calculated based on the tax rates.

[Note: Not all countries have capital gain tax. Countries like Bahrain, Barbados, Belize, Cayman Islands, Isle of Man, Jamaica, Sierra Leone, Singapore, and region like Hong Kong do not have CGT.]

The third type of income is passive income. This is income derived from business or real estate. Although this income is taxed at regular ways, there are a lot of ways to reduce the amount of income taxed. And best of all, the loss in business and real estate can be used to offset any income from the same investment activity. This is where the magic of depreciation comes in. Say, for example, Mike made an investment loss of ($26,000) in property after applying depreciation. However, he is earning 10% by investing in his friend's fish-and-chips business, which is, say, $10,000.

The loss of ($26,000) in real estate can be used to offset his $10,000. In other words, that $10,000 from his friend's fish and chips business will be tax-free. Best of all, this passive loss ($16,000) can be rolled over the next year, and so forth. This passive activity loss (PAL) of ($26,000) will continue to accumulate year after year and help offset Mike's income derived from investing in his friend's fish-and-chips business. Do you see how powerful it is? It means that all the income derived from investing in that fish-and-chips business will be tax free because of the magic of depreciation in that investment property. That is how you offset passive income with passive loss.

So, I hope you see how different incomes are subject to different tax laws. Instead of earning more income, why not earn better income? That is why tax planning is so important even before you begin to invest. To do that, you need a very good accountant.

The bottom line is that the rich don't cut their expense; they increase them. Learning how to increase your expenses to generate passive loss is one of the best-kept secrets of the rich.

Chapter 7

Beware of the Naysayer Inside You

Like many things in life, when it comes to investing, very often, all of us have a naysayer inside us. This naysayer is like a devil in our mindset. It makes excuses for us. It keeps us in our comfort zone for very good reasons. Basically, it is keeping us from our success.

I hate to tell you this. I have my own naysayer when it comes to writing the *Hidden Secrets of Investing*. I've had the idea of writing this book since I wrote my first book *Corruption of Real Money* back in 2013. But, without a S.M.A.R.T plan, I just didn't do it, not because I don't have time, and life gets in my way, but because my naysayer convinced me that I would write it *someday*. Well, that someday has been seven long years.

In life, I think there is nothing such as being too busy. If you want to finish something, you will make time, even if you don't have time.

This chapter is about saying no to the naysayer inside you.

I think that having a correct investment mindset is far more important than executing investing strategies. After all, you can know all the best investment strategies in the world but listen to the naysayer inside you and take no action at all. Listening to a naysayer will cost you opportunity cost, which you will regret later on in life.

Listen to your word

Words are very powerful tools. They determine what decision you will make. It is fair to say that every one of us is basically a summation of all the decisions we made in our life, good and bad. What life we live depends on what words we choose to use.

Words are free, but they are like a double-edged sword. If you choose your words wisely, you can kick that naysayer in your head away and dare to take on your wildest dreams. If you choose your words poorly, you will forgo a lot of opportunities.

But, how do you know it is the naysayer inside your head?

One of the most common words that a naysayer says is the word 'but.' 'But' is a very powerful word. Let me give you some examples.

"I want to learn investing, but I have no time."

"I want to buy a property, but I have no money."

"I wish to start a business, but I don't have experience."

"I want to invest in real estate, but I don't want to fix toilets."

"I want to learn about taxation, but I don't have money to take a course on it."

"I know that playing Monopoly shows you the path to true wealth, but it is not applicable to a real-life situation."

"I know that playing Cashflow 101 is going to help me to learn about investing, but the number in the game is unrealistic."

"I know I should buy positive cashflow property to be financially free, but I think the stock market might be easier for me."

And the list goes on and on.

You see my point. The word 'But' automatically shuts anyone off from accepting new ideas and allows one to make excuses. It is a very powerful word because all the excuses we make are very reasonable. They are very logical and make a lot of sense. However, this is exactly the type of thought pattern that keeps most people poor.

Instead of using the word "But," the way to counter that naysayer inside you is to ask the question, "What if?"

Let me give you some examples.

"I want to learn investing. What if I can spare an hour a day reading investment books?"

"I want to buy a property. What if I allocate $500 into my savings account every fortnight and don't touch it?"

"I wish to start a business. What if I find a mentor to guide me?"

"I want to invest in real estate, but I don't want to fix toilets. What if I find a property manager?"

"I want to learn about taxation. What if I begin by buying a book on taxation?"

"I know that playing Monopoly shows you the path to true wealth. What if I use the principle in real-life."

"I know that playing Playing Cashflow 101 is going to help me to learn about investing. What if I can emulate the lesson it teaches me in my next investment?"

"I know I should buy positive cashflow property to be financially free. What if you can teach me how to find them?"

Do you see the difference between using *"But"* and *"What if"*? One is closing the door to opportunities; another opens it with questions.

The good thing about words is that they are easy to change. Start by changing the vocabulary you are using, eliminate the word in your word of choice, and I am sure you will certainly make a difference.

Busy People are Actually Lazy

How many people do you know who are always busy but not getting anywhere in life? These people did everything right in life. They study very hard. They work very long hours. They do what their boss asks them to do. They took work home to work, doing lots of overtime. I encountered a manager who told me she couldn't even afford to take a ten-minute shower because her boss had her on international calls after work! These people work so hard that they do not have time for their wife or husband. After all, the naysayer inside their mind is working its magic to approve them.

"I want to spend more time with you and the kids, but I am really too busy right now."

To be fair, everyone has his or her own reasons. I am not criticizing if this is the right thing to do. Maybe these people have a mortgage to pay. Maybe they work so hard so that they can flip his or her property to get a decent capital gain. Maybe they have different life circumstances. Whatever this reason might be, if you are one of them, I suggest you take a break, look in the mirror, and ask yourself a simple, honest question: Am I staying busy as a way to avoid something in life? Where will this lead me one day if I keep doing what I am doing today?

Albert Einstein once said that the definition of insanity is doing the same thing over and over again and expect a different result. I cannot agree more.

If you are trying to keep yourself busy, why not try to keep track of your time? You can use the timesheet at the beginning of the book to record how you spend your time each week (See Introduction, Exercise 5). Always remember your true wealth is your time and freedom, and money is just a tool to trade your time. Instead of putting all the hours into work or Netflix, why not try to allocate one or two hours a day reading investment books, learning about tax laws, getting more financial education or starting that business you always wanted to start?

I guarantee that your life will change if you can afford to spend one to two hours each day, putting time into financial education and taking action. It is just like learning how to walk when we were babies. We can have all the good reasons to stay in that baby chair. But, once we took action and baby steps, one step at a step, we have become the person we are today.

PART III

HIDDEN SECRETS OF INVESTING

Chapter 8

Hidden Secrets of Residential Real Estate

Real Estate investing, even on a very small scale, remains a tried and true means of building an individual's cash flow and wealth

-Robert Kiyosaki

Each year, Forbes publishes a list of all the billionaires around the world. In 2020, they have listed the top 2,095 billionaires across 18 different industries. About 9% of the billionaires derived their wealth directly from real estate. Real estate is not only as good as other investments but **tens or hundreds times** better. It is the investment of the wealthy. It is the playground of the rich.

If you are beginning to chart your course in investing, there is one important rule you must remember.

REAL ESTATE CREATES WEALTH

No matter which investment vehicles you are taking, your ultimate goal is to accumulate cash flow real estate or turn your existing real estate into positive cash flow.

To begin this chapter, let me explain why I think real estate is much better than other investments.

Why Real Estate is Way Better than Other Investments?

"Ching, imagine you have $100,000 cash? How many dollars' worth of stock can you buy?" Grandad asked.

"I can buy $100,000 worth of stock," I replied. "Well, maybe more if I buy on margin...but I will have significant risk if the stock market plummets."

"Yes. Margin call. You definitely don't want to put yourself in that position. So, in nearly all cases, $100,000 cash can buy $100,000 worth of stock. Agreed?"

I nodded.

"Imagine you have $100,000 cash? How many dollars' worth of real estate can you buy?" Grandad asked.

"$100,000 worth of real estate. What's wrong?" I frowned.

"Clearly, you could do that," Grandad chuckled. "But you can also buy $500,000 worth of real estate by taking out a mortgage of 80% of the purchase price. In fact, if you are aggressive enough, you could buy $1,000,000 worth of real estate by taking out a mortgage of 90% of the purchase price."

"Do you mean real estate is much better than stock?" I frowned. "But people are doubling or tripling their money in the stock market right now."

"Markets can go up today, but they might come down tomorrow. We never know. The point is that when you buy stock, you generally have to put up the entire purchase price with your hard-earned cash. But, for real estate, the bank is begging you to take their money to invest. Now, second question. The moment you buy your $1,000,000 real estate using your $100,000 cash, how much is your property worth?"

"Of course, it is $1,000,000," I firmly replied.

"Well, let me just toss some hypotheses your way. Is it not possible that the $1,000,000 real estate you just paid for is actually worth $900,000 only? Is it possible that the real estate agent talked you into overpaying for it in auction? Is it possible that the same type of property in the surrounding area is cheaper, but you really like this one so that you overpaid?"

"I guess so...." I agreed.

"Is it also possible that the $1,000,000 real estate you just paid for is actually worth $1,100,000?" Grandad asked again.

"Impossible. How could that happen? It is too good to be true in real life," I frowned.

"It is entirely possible. In fact, it happens all the time. People sell a property below market value for various different reasons. In fact, it is easier to buy a bargain than a lemon because the bank appraisal will reflect its true value. If you think the price of a property is too good to be true, it probably is. Otherwise, you will limit yourself to ordinary deals with little or zero upside potential."

"Hmm...I am still not convinced these real estate deals exist. Who else in the world has the right mind to sell a $1,100,000 property for $1,000,000?"

"One of the most common reasons why people sell their property below the market value is divorce. You are too young to know how desperate partners want each other out of their life when things turn south in a marriage. They want their money back as soon as possible. Just sell it now, split the proceeds, and we will never see each other again."

"Apart from divorce, what are the other reasons people sell their property below the market value?"

"Well, sometimes, real estate is about people, not the actual building itself. Say, for example, if a person has financial difficulties, you would imagine that he needs money for an emergency and would like to have a quick sale. Another possibility is that someone bought that property for $100,000 in the 60s, and they think $1,000,000 is already overpriced and is too lazy to find someone for appraisal, and, therefore, sells below market value."

"Now, continuing with our example, how would you increase the value of your $100,000 stock portfolio?"

"I can't do much than to pray for the stock market stock to continue to rise over time," I replied.

"How would you increase the value of your $100,000 real estate?" Grandad smiled.

"Can we do so?" I dropped my mouth open.

"Of course, we can. We can do a lot. You can paint walls. You can install an alarm system. You can install air conditioning, a dishwasher, a dryer. You can replace the flooring. You can do any renovation you like to improve the value of your property. There are literally 101 things you can do to massively increase the value of your property. In fact, my neighbour next door just brought a house for $500,000, repainted it with a fresh coat of white paint, and resold it for $600,000. The point is, you have more control in real estate than in stock. Instead of praying the market will go up tomorrow, you can massively increase the value of your property, limited only by your imagination," Grandad explained.

"Interesting. It is very important that I am in control over my investment and don't allow that control to be handled by somebody else," I concluded.

"Exactly. Control is very important in investment. The rich are always in control of their investment. Rarely, do they allow the market to control it. How about, in a few years' time, your investment doubles in value? How will you enjoy some of the profits in your stock portfolio?" Grandad asked.

"Of course, I would sell and make a profit," I answered.

"Yes. Anyone with a stock portfolio will sell and make that capital gain. The profit will be taxed."

"But won't your profit be taxed the same way in real estate?"

"Yes. It will. But, under normal circumstances, who will sell real estate just for the sole purpose of making a profit? Real estate is an asset indexed for inflation. The rental income it generates is allowed to be indexed by increasing rent."

"But, if you don't sell, how do you ever earn that profit?" I was puzzled.

"To refinance. Say, the market goes up. That $1,000,000 property is now worth $1,500,000. You go to the bank and ask for an appraisal. Then you go to the bank to take out a new mortgage of $1,350,000. After paying back the original mortgage of $900,000, you have $450,000 cash in your hand. The best part is that this $450,000 is not taxable! It is not an income. It is not subject to capital gain tax. You can use this $450,000 as a deposit for your next property and repeat the process."

"Sounds exciting. Are there more reasons why real estate is better than stock?" I asked enthusiastically.

"Of course. Consider if you have a positive cash flow property, normally you would think that if the rental income exceeds your expenses, you will have to pay tax on the money left over." Grandad began.

"Yes. After all, it is part of my income. Then, of course, I need to pay income tax on that," I said.

Grandad shook his head.

"Do you mean this profit isn't taxable?" I pursued.

"Imagine, if you can convince the taxman that your property is actually running at a loss, will you be taxed? To understand why, you need to understand depreciation. When you buy a piece of real estate, you are not just buying the building but the building components and the land as well. While land always appreciates in value, when talking about depreciation, we are mainly talking about the building and the contents of the building. These parts of the asset go down in value over time. Because the government wants you to stay competitive, they give you the incentive to upgrade your building by allowing depreciation. Things like carpets, curtain, fittings, fixtures tend to wear down over time. But you don't need to replace them every year either. So, it costs you nothing to claim depreciation," Grandad explained.

"But how does depreciation work in reality?" I asked.

"Say, for example, you have an investment property that generates $20,000 every year. The total expenses you have are $15,000. This leaves you a net profit of $5,000. Since you know depreciation in tax laws, you did a depreciation schedule and found out that your depreciation allowance is $10,000. So, now, instead of earning passive income, you have a passive loss of $5,000. This puts you in a situation where you are actually earning $20,000 tax-free. Since the taxman sees you making a passive loss of $5,000, this loss will be used to offset your total income. Assume you have a marginal tax rate of 40%, the taxation office will refund you $2,000 in tax. What kind of investment can you name where the government will give you a check for making a loss?"

The Procedure of Buying a Property

Before I invest in my first property, I thought I should know everything about the buying procedure. However, it is not until I actually did it that

I realized how much I don't know. So, here, I think it might be valuable to share my experience with you. If you have already been through this buying stage, you can choose to skip this part. But, if you are just starting out, it might be good to use this as a guide. Since I bought my first property in Australia, the situation below might not be entirely applicable if you are in another country. Even so, the big picture is more or less the same with a little twist.

Step 1: Contract of Sale

Assume you have found a property you like; the first thing you do is to get a *contract of sale* from the real estate agent. This *contract of sale* is an important document as it is a formal agreement between the buyer and seller. You will have to send this document to your conveyancer to see if there are any potential problems in the contract. This is a very important step, as the conveyance will often see potential problems we cannot see. Do not jump into signing the *contract of sale* without your trusted conveyancer screening it. The process is free, and the conveyance will not charge you anything until you find a property you like. You will only be charged once you settle the property.

Step 2: Order a Strata Report

If you decide to go ahead, it is a wise idea to order a *strata report* for your conveyancer to check it. It might cost you a couple of hundred dollars, but it's worth every dollar. Finding out any potential problems with the property before purchasing it is crucial because you can avoid buying a property with surprising problems you cannot fix.

Step 3: Preapproval and valuation

The next step is to go to the bank for two things: Preapproval and a valuation of the property. A preapproval is pre-qualification for a loan or mortgage of a certain value range. Say, for example, your income is $100,000, you are prequalified for a mortgage of $1,000,000. So, that means you can buy any property valued at $1,250,000 if you decided to borrow 80% of the property. If you are aggressive and decided to take out a 90% mortgage, your loan to value ratio is more than 80%, and, in this case, you will have to pay lender mortgage insurance (LMI). As a very rough guide, LMI could cost over $10,000 on a home loan of $500,000. You have to check this out with your bank.

Before you apply for a loan, your bank will also require you to obtain a document called rental opinion from the real estate agent. This document is not your actual rent, but the potential rent you might receive. Beside your current income, the future rental income of your investment property will be factored into how much you can borrow as well.

Now, let's say the property you found has an asking price of $800,000. However, the bank valuation comes back and says the market value of this property is only worth $700,000. In this situation, even if your borrowing capacity is prequalified for a mortgage of $1,000,000, the bank will only lend you $560,000. (i.e. 80% x $700,000) The lending process is not only based on how much you are qualified to borrow but how much you can borrow depends on the bank's valuation. So, that's why you always need to go to the bank, ask them for a valuation of the property, sort out your finance, before you sign the *contract of sale*. If you sign the *contract of sale* first, in this case, you will have to pay that $100,000 difference. Be careful.

Step 4: Make an Offer to Put the Property Under Offer

Next, after your conveyancer and banker confirm everything, you can now begin to make an offer. Here, you have to use your negotiation skills and include any special terms and conditions you wish to include. The buying normally happens in two ways: private sale or auction. Once you make an offer in a private sale, and the offer is accepted, you will put down 0.25% deposit and sign the *contract of sale* to take the property off the market. At this point, the property is now *under offer*, and you will have five business days cooling-off period.

If you back off, you will have to pay the vendor 0.25% of the purchase price as penalty.

If everything goes smoothly, you can pay the remaining 9.75% by bank cheque to the real estate company looking after this property.

On the other hand, if the property is done through an auction, there is no cooling-off period. You have to pay 10% of the purchase price by cheque to the real estate company on the day you exchange the *contract of sale*, which is non-refundable. Either way, the total amount you need to hold a property at this point is 10% of the purchase price. Afterwards, the settlement will begin in six weeks.

Step 5: Negotiate a Good Rate and Loan

Once you have exchanged the *contract of sale*, your next task is to shop around for the best mortgage right away. The best way is to find a mortgage broker with a good reputation because he or she knows the best deal currently out there in the market. It is a good idea to pay them a visit, even though you might decide to apply for a mortgage with the bank yourself afterwards. Basically, without going into specifics, there are two types of loans: home loan (for owner occupy) and investment loan. Each of them has a fixed rate or variable rate.

A fixed rate means the interest rate is fixed for a certain period. It is usually lower than a variable rate. However, if your mortgage is fixed, you will not be able to pay the debt down, even though you have a lump sum of cash.

[Note: a loan with a fixed rate has fixed terms, which can be 1 year, 2 years, 3 years or 5 years. The fixed interest rate for different fixed terms is different. A 5-year fixed rate has a lower interest rate than a 1-year fixed rate.]

A variable rate means the interest rate is subject to market volatility. When the interest rate in the market goes up, you pay more. Conversely, if it goes down, you pay less. If your mortgage is variable rate only, you can choose to pay the debt down if you have a lump sum.

The best way, in my opinion, is to split your mortgage into half fixed, half variable. That way, you can guard against uncertainty.

Negotiating a good interest rate is very important, as this will affect your cashflow. Do your own due diligence. Shop around and find a banker or mortgage broker who is willing to work in your favour. Some mortgage brokers will try to convince you to cross-collateralize your property; my suggestion for you is don't. Cross-collateralizing your property is a bad start if you want to build a property portfolio. Cross-collateralization allows you to use a property to secure a loan or multiple loans without using any of your own funds. But if one property in the portfolio has enjoyed a capital gain and the others have dropped in value, the net effect on the total value may be zero. Also, you are scarifying a lot of flexibility in equity assessment, and every property in a cross-collateralised portfolio needs to be re-valued whenever one property is released.

For both home loans and investment loans, you can choose to have an *interest only loan*. Unlike a typical home loan, where you have to pay down the principal and interest, an *interest only loan* requires you to pay down the interest component only. It means there is less repayment each month, but the principal you owe will never go down. Depending on your investment strategy, in some cases, an interest only loan is really powerful. It can turn your negative cashflow property into positive cashflow. But, just don't use an *interest only loan* if you are trying to pay off your own home loan.

Before you complete applying for a mortgage, you have to make sure the mortgage you apply can be linked to an offset account. This is an important step. Unlike a savings account, funds in an offset account do not earn interest. They are used to reduce the interest costs on the loan. So, if your loan is an *interest only loan*, an offset account can reduce your monthly repayment. If your loan is to repay both principal and interest, an offset account will not reduce your monthly repayment but reduces the duration it takes you to pay off your mortgage. Setting up your offset account is free, costs you nothing, and all you have to do is to talk to your bank.

Once the mortgage application is approved and successful, your bank will inform you that they are ready to settle your loan. At this point, you need to inform your conveyancer of your settlement date.

Step 6: Legal
During these six weeks, there will be a lot of communication with your conveyancer. Your conveyancer will ask you to confirm the *contract of sale*. He or she will need you to fill in a list of documents like the *Purchaser Declaration Form* and *Client Authorization Form* to act on your behalf.

He or she will also request you to order title insurance, which is a couple of hundred dollars, depending on the price of your property.

If you purchase the property as a couple, your conveyance will ask if you want to own the property as *Joint Tenants* or *Tenants in Common* (I will explain the differences later in the legal section).

Afterwards, he or she will ask if you would like to order government enquiries to see what the government's present and future activities are in the area.

Next, he or she will need to check your identity as part of the government's enquiry. Some conveyancers will be able to check your identity for you as part of the service. If not, your conveyancer will tell you how to book it online.

Lastly, your conveyancer will also remind you of the penalty if you cannot settle on the settlement date as well as to confirm when and how much your stamp duty is. Apart from that, your conveyancer will do a lot of background work like checking for outstanding arrears or land tax obligations, calculate adjustments for council and water rates and find out if the government authority has a vested interest in the area like property development.

Two weeks prior to settlement, your conveyancer will contact you again to arrange a final inspection with the real estate agent to make sure the condition of the property is as stated in the contract. During the final inspection, it is very important you have a checklist in hand to document and photograph everything you want to fix prior to settlement. If you skip this step, after settlement, you have to pay out of your pocket to have them fixed.

One week before the settlement, your conveyance will send you an email detailing all the costs payable. He or she will also send you a settlement adjustment sheet, detailing the outstanding council rates, strata levies, water & sewerages rate, water usage and strata 184 certificates, etc. Do allow an extra $1,000 to cover this. Apart from that, there will be a *transfer registration fee* (a legal document that transfers the ownership of property into your name), which costs about one hundred, *mortgage registration fee* (mortgage registration ensures that the mortgage can be viewed by a simple title search.), which costs another one hundred, and, of course, the conveyancing fee.

Step 7: Settlement

Two days prior to the settlement day, all you need to do is to prepare the remaining 10% of the purchase price and the stamp duty in your nominated bank account.

On the settlement date, the bank, your conveyancer and the seller's conveyance will do everything in the background. You don't need to do anything. When the settlement finishes, all you need to do is to go to the real estate agent to get your keys.

Before you Begin Your Real Estate Journey

I hope that by now, you are convinced why real estate is the best investment among all asset classes, and you are confident about the buying process.

Prior to investing, you must have a plan. This plan is your roadmap in your investing journey. This chapter is about real estate. But real estate is only an investment vehicle to get you from point A to point B. So, before you begin to invest, please write down your S.M.A.R.T goals and money rules. Always remember, if you don't have a rule on money, the money will rule you.

This chapter is divided into different sections.

- The Real Estate Formula
- The Property Cycle
- Creative Finance
- Property Strategies

I will take you through a helicopter ride about possible ways you can get into real estate investing. Please be advised that the subject in this chapter can be intimidating, and it may be difficult to understand every strategy in one go. But don't worry as this book is designed to be an easy read. You might need to refer back to the strategies from time to time, twist it and apply it to your own financial situation. If you are ready, let's begin our journey.

The Real Estate Formula

Unlike investing in other asset classes, investing in real estate is somehow repetitive and, to be honest, a bit boring. You will follow the same procedure for every deal you make. This book is NOT about buying any real estate. There are plenty of books on the market that teach you so. The hidden secret of this chapter is about teaching you the techniques to assemble a *real estate deal* with high return. I believe that the real value in real estate investing is NOT actually the real estate itself but the *real estate deal* you assemble as an investor. Your ultimate goal is to buy investment property below market value that has a high return.

So, to begin your real estate journey, you must follow these 7 steps like a formula:

1)   Market Research
2)   Analyze Deals
3)   Negotiation

4)   Finance

5)   Legal

6)   Due Diligence

7)   Property Management

Market Research

To begin, familiarize yourself with the real estate activities in two or three potential areas only. Each area can be made up of one or several suburbs. Try not to look at more than three areas because you will lose focus and eventually end up not going anywhere. Focusing on three areas will make things manageable. The purpose of market research is to be a market expert in these three areas, which means you will know the following in that suburb:

1.   Market trends.

2.   Location.

3.   The market value of each type of property (i.e., unit, apartment, villa, townhouse, house, duplex, etc.).

4.   The demand and supply of each type of property.

5.   How many people are likely to rent each type of property.

6.   Employment.

7.   Demographics.

8.   Population.

9.   Vacancy rate.

10.   Growth rate.

11.   Government activities and plans.

To choose an area, find out about its past growth rate. You want to choose an area with a growth rate of at least 10% over the past decade. Look for evidence that the area has experienced property growth. Look out for signs of rapid growth for suburbs in these areas in the last 2-3 years. Find out what caused the growth.

However, skip these suburbs, as these suburbs have already experienced growth. You want to look out for their neighbour suburbs, as they will benefit from the spill-over effect of high growth suburbs and experience potential growth. Nowadays, there are many property market research websites like *Pricefinder* or *RP data* that will have these data.

Once you have identified those suburbs you want to invest in, the next step is to observe its proximity for convenience, transport, lifestyle, and education. Properties in school catchment areas are usually in high demand. They will attract good tenants and investors. Choose a suburb within 10km of a major financial hub, as this is proximity to employment. If there are government projects in the area you chose, like a subway, it will increase your value over the long run.

In addition, you also want to find out about the rental yield and vacancy rate of the chosen area. You want to find an area with a rental yield of 5% or higher and a vacancy rate of less than 2%. Find out what type of property has a limited supply. If an area has population growth but a limited supply of property, you will more likely to have high demand.

Next, further streamline yourself into finding out the most profitable *streets*. Not all streets have the same value. It is just like the game, Monopoly, where properties in some street always have a higher value than others. It depends on many factors like whether it is a school catchment area, quite close to parks and public transport, etc. Go to these highlighted streets and observe the properties. Are these new or old properties? Are they mainly houses or units?

To know more about the suburb, the best and fastest way is to talk to local real estate agents and the friendly neighbourhoods. Real estate agents are like your eyes and ears. If you have developed a good relationship with them, they will tell you a lot about the local market, or even deals that haven't come to the market yet. Work with agents who are real estate investors themselves, as they speak the same language as you. Once in a while, if you are lucky, you might stumble into a real estate agent that might offer you an off-market sell. So, why not build a connection with them.

Lastly, you will need to narrow down the type of property in these streets. Your ultimate goal is to find properties that are selling below the market value. One of the ways to do that is to pay attention to the properties in a suburb that have been listed for more than three months. If a property has been listed for a very long time, the real estate agent is likely to work in your favour. In the real estate agent's position, if they don't sell a property, they will never get the commission no matter how hard they work. So, in a situation like this, they are more likely to convince the seller to lower their expectation.

The market research phase is so important that you do not want to skip it. But the best thing is that you only need to do it once. Once you become a market expert in your areas, knowing if a property is selling below market value will become like an instinct to you.

Analysis Deals

Once you have found a property, your next step is to analyze the deal in the following five steps.

1.   Verify the income of the property.

2.   Verify the expenses of the property.

3.   Determine the net operating income.

4.   Find out the Capitalization Rate and Valuation.

5.   Calculate loan payment.

6.   Find out the cash on cash return.

The trick is to use these steps to come up with the initial cash flow and work backwards towards the price you want to offer. In good deals, the numbers work. In bad deals, it doesn't. The seller's asking price is irrelevant because the number must work out for you, not for them.

The income of your property is obviously your rental income. What most people don't realize is that there are actually four other types of income through real estate. They are:

1.   Rental income

2.   Depreciation

3.   Amortization

4.   Appreciation (appreciation of real estate value over time)

The expenses of properties fluctuate over time. Property has several expenses, namely:

Costs of owning the property:

•   Body corporate fees

•   Borrowing and mortgage-related expenses

•   Capital works costs (associated with construction costs on the investment)

•   Depreciation on assets within the property (eg., in-built electrical appliances)

•   Loans relating to the property

•   Insurance costs

•   Pest control

•   Depreciation report costs

•   Council rates

•   Land tax

- Repairs to property (once initial occupation has commenced)
- Travel-related expenses when accessing the property for repairs and inspection

Costs of tenanting:

- Advertising fees
- Cleaning costs
- Agent commission and management fees
- Electricity and gas costs when property unoccupied
- Gardening costs
- Letting fees
- Legal fees associated with tenant dispute resolution
- Landlord insurance

Costs of administering investment:

- Accountant fees
- Postage costs
- Stationary costs
- Bookkeeping fees
- Bank charges

The Net Operating Income (NOI) tells an investor how profitable the income generating calculated by the formula:

Net Operating Income = Rental Income – Operating Expense

NOI is a before tax figure. So, it excludes mortgage repayment, depreciation, and amortization.

When investing in real estate, one of the things a real estate investor must keep in mind is how to raise the NOI. To do so, you must think of ways to add value to the property. When you add value to the property, you can increase the rent. One example is when you find a decent property that doesn't have a dishwasher or dryer, you can consider making them an addition. You can depreciate these items over time, and, at the same time, you can increase occupancy, increase the rental income and improve the NOI and the value of the property. Later on, you can refinance the property to get back the cost. Adding building contents and depreciate those contents is a formula you might want to incorporate into your investing plan.

Another important concept is the Capitalization Rate (*Cap Rate*), which is the ratio of the NOI to the property value. Say, for example, a property is sold for $500,000 with an NOI of $15,800; it has a *Cap Rate* of 3.16%. It is good to look for areas with a high market cap rate.

$$Capitalization\ Rate = \frac{NOI}{Property\ Value}$$

But why is *Cap Rate* important?

Cap Rate is a barometer for you to work out the *valuation* of your property in order to be able to refinance to extract equity.

The loan payment of your property can be calculated using the bank's mortgage repayment tool. Nowadays, most banks offer a mortgage repayment calculator that allows you to select a mortgage plan and work out the repayment.

Analyzing property deals become very mechanical once you become a seasonal investor. The best way to do this is to implement these formulas in an Excel spreadsheet. By doing so, it can save you a lot of time and allow you to filter out profitable deals very quickly.

Negotiation

The truth is that you will not always find property that is selling below the market value. But, if you negotiate the price well, the property deal will still be profitable. Remember that real estate investing is also about people, not just about the piece of the asset. And if you can find out why the vendor is selling, this will give you a better position in negotiation. It may surprise you that not everyone is selling because they need the money.

Different people sell property for different reasons. Some of them are desperate for a quick sale. Some do not. I will discuss how to create a profitable real estate deal later in this chapter.

One of the easiest ways to find property selling below market value is to look at those properties that have been listed for more than three months. If the property has been on the market for a long time, the real estate agent will start to lose belief in the property. Remember, real estate agents only get paid when the property is sold. They do not get paid for doing overtime. That means their commission does not vary very much if they sell the property for the asking price or 10% below. The quicker they sell the property and move on to the next deal, the better. Show them evidence with your market research that the property is worth the asking price. But, at the same time, be a good listener. Be patient. A good negotiator solves problems and puts everyone in a win-win situation.

Finance

The most crucial component in real estate investing is probably equity.

When you bought a property of $500,000 with 20% down payment, which is $100,000, that $100,000 becomes your equity. And when your property appreciates to $550,000, and you paid down your debt to $350,000, your equity becomes $200,000. In a nutshell, equity is the current home price minus the debt owed to the bank. You can use equity as a deposit to buy further property.

Equity = property value - outstanding loan amount

The bank decides how much you can borrow by looking at the Loan to Value ratio (LVR), which is simply the home loan or investment loan amount divided by the value of your property.

Normally, the bank accepts an LVR of 80%. If you go above that threshold, you will need to pay lender mortgage insurance (LMI). LMI is a one-off, non-refundable, non-transferrable premium that's added to your home loan. LMI is designed to protect the bank if you are unable to pay your loan. Depending on your strategy and circumstances, sometimes, LMI is worth paying if the property price rises quicker than you can save up for a deposit.

Legal

The legal part of real estate is probably the most overlooked part of the real estate investing process. When you buy the property with one or more people, you will have to state whether you are holding the property as *Joint Tenants* or *Tenants in Common*.

If you own the property as *Joint Tenants*, this means you own the property in equal share. If one owner dies, then their share will automatically pass on to the other owners. This type of legal structure is best suited for couples.

If you own the property as *Tenants in Common*, you can choose to own the property in equal shares or unequal share, say 1/3 or 2/3. When one owner dies, the Will of that person will decide who gets the ownership share. It will not automatically go to the other co-owners as it would if you held it as *Joint Tenants*. This type of legal structure is best suited for business partners or friends.

[Note: In the contract, always ask your conveyancer to include a clause - subject to finance. A subject to finance clause tells the vendor (property seller) that you legally agree to the purchase on the condition that you receive formal home loan approval.]

Due Diligence

Due diligence is about doing your homework about the interior of the property and its location. Do it right, and you'll be in great shape. I have seen a lot of investors skip due diligence and burned themselves when they discovered the hidden costs after settlement, so don't be one of them.

Due diligence is the careful evaluation of a potential investment to confirm all material facts. In a nutshell, do your homework.

For example, getting a strata report is due diligence. A strata report tells you the existing condition of the property. They tell you if the property has structural issues or problems like water leakage from the roof. Once you discover those hidden costs, you can always go back to the vendor to negotiate the price down.

A good investor always does his or her due diligence. The more detail you are able to do this, the better. When I got my first property, my uncle taught me to look out for the number of holes in bricks, as this tells you about the age of the property. Old homes usually have three holes. New ones have sixteen. The brick manufacturer increases the number of holes in the brick because they want to save transportation costs by cutting down weight. As a rule of thumb, the less holes there are on a brick, the more solid, thus, better quality. That is why older homes tend to have fewer problems than new homes. There are too many horror stories in shaking apartment buildings today because developers want to save costs at the expense of structural integrity. In the worst case, owners and tenants are forced to evacuate because the apartment buildings might collapse.

Other times, you need to check the history and the environmental report of a suburb. It might have problems that you don't realize and cannot be fixed. Look out for suburbs that have been an industrial zone previously, and there is a high risk of water contamination. Look out for suburbs where there are potential sinking problems of land. If you discover those problems after you have bought the property, it will be a huge mistake. These problems will severely affect the growth of the property. Worst of all, it is very hard to sell property with those problems.

Below is an example of due diligence checklists. Go through each item carefully. If you have questions, bring it to the accountant and conveyancer to review the deal.

1)   Current rent roster with paid to dates

2)   List of security deposits

3)   Mortgage payment information

4)   Personal property list

5)   Floor plans

6)   Insurance policy, agent

7)   Maintenance, service agreement

8)   Tenant information: leases, ledger cards, applications, smoke detector forms

9)   List of vendors and utility companies, including account numbers

10)   A statement of structural alterations made to the premises

11)   Surveys and engineering documents

12)   Commission agreements

13)   Rental or listing agreements

14)   Easement agreements

15)   Development plans, including plans and specifications, and as-built architectural, structural, mechanical, electrical, and civil drawings

16)   Governmental permits or zoning restrictions affecting the development of the property

17)   Management contracts

18)   Tax bills and property tax statements

19)   Utility bills

20)   Cash receipts and disbursement journals pertaining to the property

21)   Capital expenditure disbursement records pertaining to the property for the last five years

22)   Income-and-expense statements pertaining to the property for two years prior to the submission date

23)   Financial statements and state and federal tax returns for the property

24)   A termite inspection in form and content reasonably satisfactory to the buyer

25)   All other records and documents in the Seller's possession or under the Seller's control, which would be necessary or helpful to the ownership, operation, or maintenance of the property

26)   Market surveys or studios of the area

27)   Construction budget or actuals

28)   Tenant profiles or surveys

29)   Work-order files

30)   Bank statements for two years showing the operating account for property

31)   Certificate of Occupancy

32)   Title abstract

33)   Copies of all surviving guarantees and warranties

34)   Phase I Environmental Audit (if it exists)

Besides that, it is also important to check the interior and the exterior of the property and record all damages you see for negotiation.

List of photos recommended:

1)   Exterior photos of the building

2)   Photos of the entrance

3)   Photo of all bedrooms

4)   Photos of all bathrooms

5)   Photos of the kitchen

6)   Photo of the living space

7)   Photos of the garage

8)   Photo of the outdoor area

9)   Photo of all fixtures and fittings, tiles, door handles, flooring, light, carpet and curtain, etc.

10)   Photos of anything that need to be repaired

11)   Photo of water drainage

12)   Photo of the ceiling for cracks and watermark

13)   Photo of the laundry

14)   Photos of the look of each window

15)   Check all keys are there, and if they are working

16)   Photos of all appliances (dishwater, dryer, hot water system, air conditioning, etc.)

Property Management

After you have successfully bought the property, you are going to rent it out. The next thing to do is to find a professional real estate company to manage the property for you. Most agencies charge 7%-12% plus GST for property management fee. But, this is worth their fee many times over because they are going to do jobs like:

- Advertising the property

- Finding tenants

- Chasing rent

- Deposit bonds

- Coordinating repairs (e.g., fixing toilets)

- Doing property inspection

- Attending tenancy tribunal

Instead of spending time on these, getting a good real estate agent that manages your property can save you both time and money. Imagine you have a property portfolio of 10 to 15 properties in the future, how can you manage all the properties by yourself? Instead of spending time to manage the property, leave it to the professionals. The fee you pay them is worth it because you can spend more time looking for more deals instead of juggling the day-to-day task of managing the properties. Best of all, agent fees are tax deductible.

Beware of The Property Cycle

There is a saying in Australia that property value doubles every seven to ten years. The truth is that in reality, some suburbs do, and some don't. It really depends on which part of the cycle you bought your property.

Opportunity Phase

Correction
Phase

Growth Phase

Peak Phase

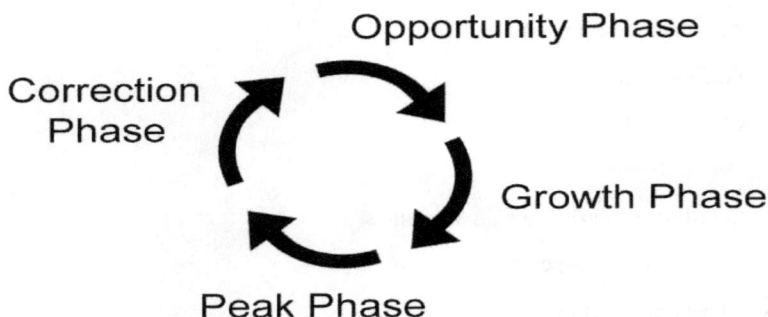

Figure 8.1: Property Cycle

Source: Author

Short-term, the real estate market tends to be psychological. But, long-term, it behaves in a cycle. In a country like Australia, we have different states. Interestingly, they all have their own property cycle. Knowing which part of the property cycle you are in in each state gives you an advantage to build your portfolio faster.

But, what is a property cycle anyway?

A property cycle has four major phases:

1)   Opportunity Phase

2)   Growth Phase

3)   Peak Phase

4)   Correction Phase

An opportunity phase is when the real estate market has just collapsed. This was when many investors got burnt. During this phase, the sediment in real estate is low. Everyone will share his or her story on how bad real estate investment is. This is usually the time you can snap off a lot of opportunity in the market.

The growth phase is what the market sediment picks up. Investors begin to jump back into the market again.

In the peak phase, everyone jumps on the real estate boat once again. Real estate makes headlines on a daily basis. Even a taxi driver will tell you how great real estate investing is.

And the last phase is the correction phase; this is when recession happens, people have trouble holding their overpriced real estate and panic sell.

Most people would think the correction phase is the best buying time.

I was one of them. However, experience has proven me wrong.

If you are a first home buyer, my advice is don't try to time the market. You will be disappointed. If you wait too long, the price of inaction far outweighs wrong timing. Let me give you a contradictory example. Hong Kong had a property crash in 1997, the market peak at 1997 and began to decline until 2003. The correction phase lasted for a long six years. Imagine you bought right at the peak, you will have most likely resulted in negative equity, meaning your mortgage is worth more than the value of your property. The reason why I hold off my property purchase since I graduated is that I apply the same logic in Australia as if I were in Hong Kong.

Below is a chart showing the Hong Kong property cycle. If you look at the chart below, the opportunity phase of the Hong Kong property market started in the early 80s. And the growth phase happened from 1985 to 1997. In 1997, we have the peak phase, followed by a 6- year correction phase. Do you see why I say don't advise to time the market? Imagine you are a graduate in 1984 at the age of 23, and finally saved up a few years for a deposit in 1987 when you are 26, then you decided to wait because the market was way too high compared to a few years ago. At some point, you will be priced out of the market between 1987 to 1997. That is a decade of wait. By the time you've finally waited for that peak, you'll be 36. And if you get older, the bank is less likely to allow you to take out a 30-year mortgage compared to when you are in your 20s. Even if the banks allowed it, the price of property in the next property cycle (2003 – present) is always higher than the growth phase of 1987.

Hang Seng Index vs. HK Residential Property Price Index

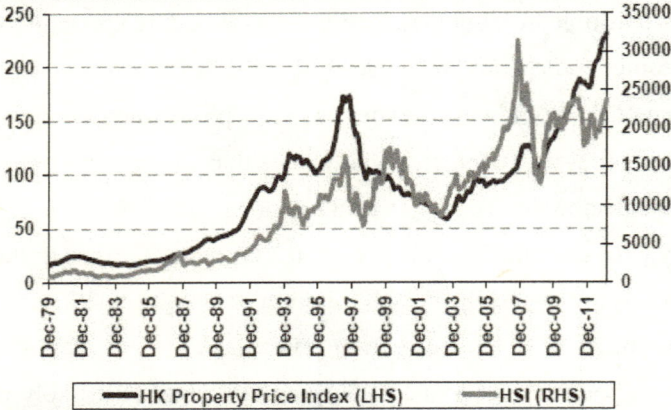

Source: HSI Company, CEIC, Morgan Stanley Research, monthly data as of January 2013.

Figure 8.2: Hong Kong Home Price

Source: HIS Company, CEIC, Morgan Stanley Research

In addition, during the correction phase, the bank is less likely to lend. It is far more difficult to get a loan during the correction phase than in the growth phase. Unless you have a lump sum of cash, it is very difficult to take advantage of the correction phase.

If you look into the global house price index, you will realize the duration of different phases in different countries can be very different. Their last property cycle looks like an opportunity phase compared to the new property cycle happening today, except for one country – Japan.

Global house price index
Q1 1980 =100

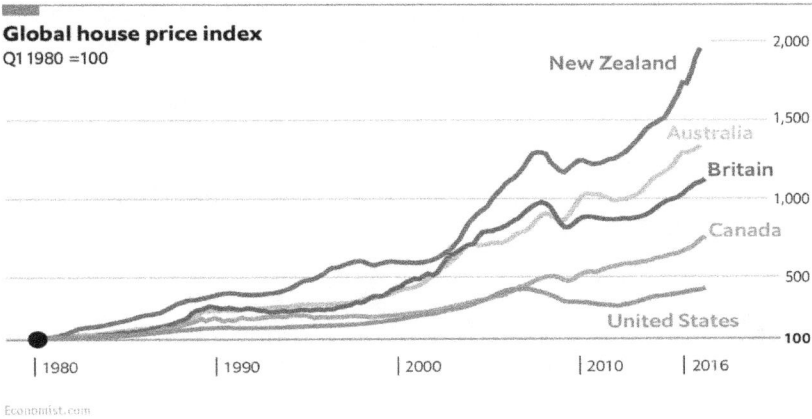

Figure 8.3: Global House Price Index

Source: Economist.com

Japan's property market peaked by the end of the 80s. It was once said that the land price of Japan had risen to a level that the land price of the Imperial Garden in Tokyo was said to be more than the State of California! The price tripled from 1984 Q4 to 1987 Q4 during the growth phase, and the long-term correction phase has lasted to even today. Even at a zero percent interest rate, property prices stay flat.

RESIDENTIAL PROPERTY PRICE INDEX - TOKYO METROPOLITAN AREA, 1984-2018
2010 = 100

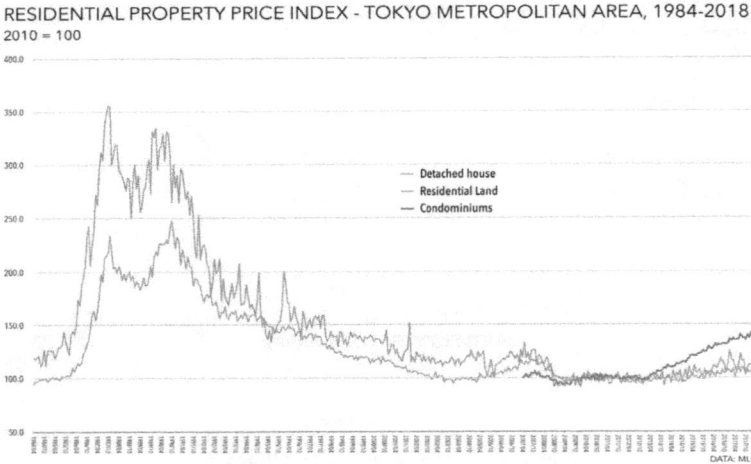

Figure 8.4: Residential Property Price Index of Tokyo

Source: MUT

So, you see, there is no definite timeframe for each phase of the property cycle. Some countries can have a correction phase that lasts 25 years, while others can experience this within six months.

Will what happened to Japan ever happen to your country?

Sure, it could happen. But there are too many driving forces behind growth and collapse. Factors like migration, employment, capital flight, aging population, employment, supply and demand of property, the banks' lending policy, a huge influx of money from a country like China all play a very important role in your property market. My point is that the probability of a Japan-style deflationary collapse is low, and the opportunity cost you have missed by waiting for a collapse is not worth it.

Instead of waiting for a peak, your strategy should be to buy property once you have saved up for a deposit. Repeat this process as quickly as possible. Time is money. Sure, you will have risk. The real estate market tends to be psychological in the short-term. But even if you buy in a dip in the first two or three years, the price rise in the decade ahead will dwarf any bad timing decision you made in the present.

Creative Finance

In reality, some of you reading right now might have difficulty entering the market. Unlike our parent's generation, property prices around the world have risen many times in the past few decades. In places like Hong Kong, unless you have sugar parents who are willing to support you, it is very difficult to get into the real estate market using conventional investing methods.

Unfortunately, this trend will only continue.

If finance is what holds you back in getting into real estate, then the creative finance in this section is going to be an eye-opener for you. I really want you to be able to accumulate wealth through real estate after reading this book. If you can do so, then I have done my job in showing you the path to true wealth. Like Robert Kiyosaki, the author of *Rich Dad Poor Dad* says, real estate investing, even on a very small scale, remains a tried and true means of building an individual's cash flow and wealth.

Vendor Finance

Conventionally, to get into real estate, you either need to save up for a 20% down payment or have sufficient equity in existing properties to get into a deal.

But what if you are caught in a situation where you want to get into the market, but you have not saved up enough deposit for your first property?

That is where *vendor finance* comes into play.

Let's say, there is a property that costs $1,000,000, and you work out you can profit $300,000 after you have renovated it. In order to buy it, you need a deposit of $300,000. The bank will finance you the remaining $700,000.

But $300,000 is a huge sum of money to save, even without taking the stamp duty into account. By the time you save enough, the property is going to be higher already.

Vendor finance can help you in this case. Vendor finance means the vendor who is selling the property gives you money to buy the property for you. Instead of saving up $300,000, get *vendor finance* to finance your deposit.

Sounds ridiculous, right?

Why on earth would the vendors pay you to buy their property?

Here is how you get it to work. Instead of paying $1,000,000 for the asking price of the property, you tell the vendor you will pay them $1,100,000. That means you have to reduce your profit by $100,000. You will negotiate a deal with the vendor that you will pay them $700,000 first, and in 12 months' time, you will pay them the rest. In 12 months' time, your development is completed, and you will sell the property for a profit or refinance. The condition is, the vendor must finance your $300,000 deposit.

If you think *Vendor finance* doesn't happen, look again. *Vendor finance* happens a lot in real estate development. And you can borrow this technique as part of your investment strategy. For example, you can use *Vendor finance* for a house that you can see potential upside in value in 12 months' time after renovation. Depending on the vendor, *Vendor finance* might not work all the time. But the point is, you only need to find a vendor who is willing to make this work for you. To find that vendor, you must keep trying and submit more offers. Eventually, if you find one that actually wishes to do this type of deal, you'll be able to afford the deposit instead of waiting years to save up to get into the property market. Find a property, work out how you can add value, and work out the numbers of how much profit you will make. Make sure you can pay that $700,000 mortgage within the 12 months of vendor finance. Find enough reasons for vendors to offer vendor finance. And you will be able to create a win-win situation.

Option

A property option is the *right but not the obligation to purchase a property within a predetermined time period at an agreed price.*

It is the same concept as a lay-by, where a buyer and seller agree on a fixed sale price and payment conditions of a product.

In a lay-by agreement, the seller will hold the goods until the customer finalises the payments. Any agreed deposit paid by the consumer is an instalment. During this period, the seller does not charge the buyer interest on the outstanding debt. The seller and the buyer are free to decide on the lay-by period, which can be anything from one week to many months. The seller may impose a cancellation fee if a consumer decides to cancel a lay-by agreement.

An option contract works like a lay-by agreement on property. You do not own the property. You are buying the *right to purchase the property,* but not the property itself. An option allows you to lock the property away from the rest of the market so that no one else can buy that property for the period of time.

But, why would any seller accept an option contract?

Let's look at an example below.

Let's say you drive around and find a site that has a house on it on the left and a free block of land on the right. This beautiful block of land has development potential. If you can build another house on the right, you can massively increase the value of the site.

Before executing this strategy, you need development approval (DA), which costs $10,000, depending on the complexity of your project. A DA approval takes 6 to 12 months to do. Once it is done and approved by the council, it can increase the value of the property before the property is even built. With this DA, the site with a house and a block of land on it will not only be worth $500,000 but $650,000. Property developers are usually willing to pay a premium to buy property with a DA because it reduces the risk for them for the uncertainty to get the DA done. With a DA, they can start building straight away.

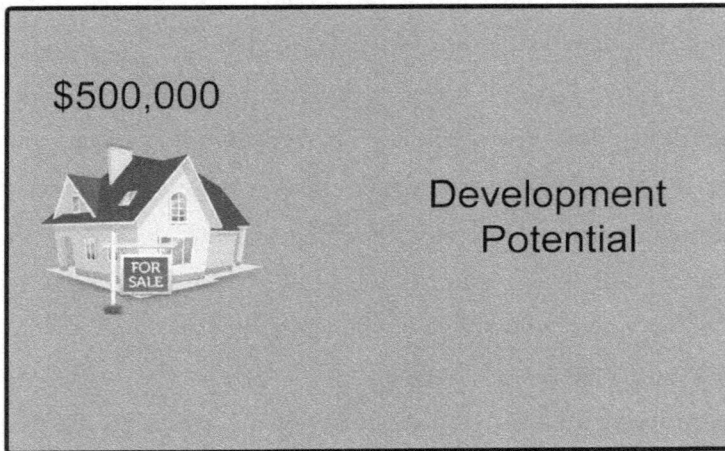

Figure 8.5: Residential Property Price Index of Tokyo

Source: MUT

On the other hand, if you buy the property without an option, you will begin to pay interest on your mortgage, the stamp duty, and, at the same time, wait for the DA to be approved; this will quickly eat up the cost of your $150,000. ($650,000 - $500,000).

By using a property option, which typically costs around $1,500 to $2,000, you have the right but not the obligation to buy the property. You can eliminate all the associated costs with buying a property. If you don't have a job, don't worry. No deposit. No worries. Bad credit rating. No worries. Creating an option contract to have this right doesn't need any of these criteria.

Here is how you make money in property using options.

Step one: Tell the owner you want to buy the property, and you want to use an option deal. In the seller's perspective, he will be receiving the $1,500 to $2,000 on top of the asking price of the property. But, instead of settling right away, he will settle it in one years' time. During this period, your outgoing cost is the option fee and the cost of doing a DA, which is $12,000.

Step two: approach a developer to buy the option from you to have the right to develop, which is $150,000. You will make $138,000 in a 12-month period by being a deal maker, profiting from a property you never owned. The developer is going to build this property and even make more money from it. This is how everyone wins in this situation.

Joint Venture

Syndicate is a property investment strategy, where multiple buyers pool their money together to buy a property they couldn't afford on their own. For example, Peter saw a $550,000 property investment in a suburb that has an uprise potential because of government development. He has the borrowing capacity, but he just hasn't saved enough for deposit. His Uncle, Joe, on the other hand, has the deposit but lacks the borrowing capacity because he bought too many negative geared properties. This is where joint venture comes in.

To make this deal possible, Peter will assemble a syndicate deal with his uncle. In the syndicate contract, his uncle will be a money partner while Peter is the equity partner. His uncle will put down the 20% and stamp duty, and Peter will borrow 80% from the bank. They structure in their agreement to have 50-50 ownership. Their plan is to sell the property in a few years' time after it has appreciated.

The beautiful thing about joint venture is that you can get into the deal much quicker that's otherwise impossible to do so.

In a syndicate, there can be three types of partners.

1.   Money Partner (Offer deposit and down payment)

2.   Equity Partner (Offer equity)

3.   Experience Partner (Offer time and experience)

In fact, a syndicate is a very common tool that the rich use to structure a deal. Each partner in a syndicate deal leverages the other partners' time, money, debt or experience for a win-win.

Before you do a syndicate deal, you have to make sure of the role and responsibility of each partner. You have to talk to your solicitor on how to properly structure a syndicate deal. You have to work out the right split among investors. However, every partner needs to have an exit strategy if things do not go according to plan.

In the 21st century, "generation rent" has become a growing breed. This situation will only get worse as the price of real estate around the globe continues to rise due to population growth. Renters are expected to spend at least 40% of their income on rent. As the cost of living continues to rise, many young people born in the 21st century will be priced out of the market. That's why I think creative finance strategies like joint venture will help anyone who has trouble saving for the deposit or a low income earner to enter the property market. If you have decided to do a joint venture, find a trustworthy partner for the deal you want to make. Make sure that you both sign a watertight legal agreement to protect your interests.

Gift Equity

Imagine there is a way where you can skip saving up year after year for a deposit. If you fall into this group, then this creative finance strategy called Gift Equity might interest you.

Gift Equity doesn't really means it is a gift. You still need to work for it. But, instead of saving up for years, you save it in another way. Let me give you an example. Consider a real estate developer just finished his 40-unit block. He is desperate to sell it quickly for a profit. As a property deal maker, you go to him and help him out. Negotiate with the property developer that you are going to sell some of his property for him without charging him agent fees or a marketing fee. At the same time, you are also eager to buy one of his properties as well. Instead of him paying you the agent fee or marketing fee, the developer fee, the profit of every sale you made will be counted towards the deposit for the property you want to buy from him.

From a developer's perspective, they want to take the stock off their hand even before the property is finished. Developing properties is a very cash-intensive business. Very often, developers sell their properties *off the plan*, meaning they sell a property that hasn't yet been built. By helping developers finding potential buyers to earn gift equity, you are saving yourself years to acquire a deposit. It is one of the best ways because you can also enjoy the potential capital growth of the *off the plan* property and acquire it with none of your own money.

[Note: To do this deal, you are required to have a real estate agent license.]

Property Strategies

When we invest in property, the conventional way is to *buy and hold*. While buy and hold is one of the best strategies to use, very often, you need to wait for years for the equity to go up. Besides the ones I talk about below, I am going to show you other property strategies where you can apply in real estate investing.

- Renovation
- Subdivision
- Splitter

Renovation

Do you wonder why some real estate investors tend to buy old or ugly properties?

While this type of property might look like trash to some real estate investors, renovators see them as gold. Real estate investors, who love renovation projects, are active investors. They usually buy *old houses in a good location*. This breed of investor tends to pick old houses because the house has a land component attached to it, which always appreciates in value. They choose old houses because there are a lot of rooms to increase the value.

Most of the time, skilled renovators see value where passive real estate investors do not.

There are three types of renovation strategies: *renovate to sell, renovate to rent and renovate to extract equity.*

Before any renovation, you must be clear about what the associated cost is. How much does it cost to renovate the bathroom and the kitchen? How much value can you add by putting in an extra wall to add a room in the property? How much equity can you manufacture by adding a carport?

Should you hire a professional to do the renovation? How much value can you add by retiling or repainting? During a real estate seminar I attended, my mentor gave me an example of how a real estate investor upvalued his property by $100,000 simply by repainting the exterior of the property with a fresh coat of white paint! In real estate, there are a lot of ways where you can massively increase the value of a property at a fraction of a cost.

Also, it is worth noting that there are two types of renovations: cosmetic renovation and structural renovation.

Cosmetic renovation, like repainting, is the type of renovation recommended. Never buy a property that needs structural renovation. By changing the structure of the property, you will require a structural engineer to assess your structural change, which is an additional cost and needs time for development approval. You want the cosmetic renovation to be done as soon as possible because the quicker you finish, the quicker you can resell for a higher profit or extract equity for your next investment property.

To do a renovation, simply work out how much you will profit and how much time is needed for the project. Then work backwards to do a feasibility assessment. For the sake of simplicity, say you bought the property for $450,000, negotiate the price down to $400,000. The cost of renovation costs $44,000, and the holding cost of the property is 2 months, which costs $6,000 in interest repayments. Finally, once you have completed the renovation, you revalue it for $650,000. In this case, you manufactured $200,000 equity. (i.e. $650,000 - $400,000 - $44,000 - $6,000)

Renovation is active property investing. It will help to actively squeeze equity out of the property quicker than the *buy and hold strategy*. Even so, it is not that renovation is better than buy and hold. I see people lose money in a renovation or end up breaking even after months of hard work. That is why you need to do your own due diligence and understand the numbers very well.

[**Note**: It is worth mentioning that there are three types of construction in property: Double Brick, Brick Veneer and timber. Double brick property has internal and external walls constructed in bricks. They are much more stable and have better insulation in heat. A double brick house is the most expensive one. Brick Veneer has the same visual aesthetic appeal as double brick, but actually, it only has a single brick wall supported by a timber frame covered with a lining material. It doesn't have the same thermal insulation like double brick. Timber construction has the least visual aesthetic appeal. However, it is the cheapest among all three types of property construction.]

Subdivision

Subdivision is a property development strategy where it is possible to generate a great chunk of cash. It involves buying a property on a large block of land, say 800m^2, and then subdividing it into two lots. The concept is simple; however, you must go to the local council as there are regulations governing what you can and cannot do.

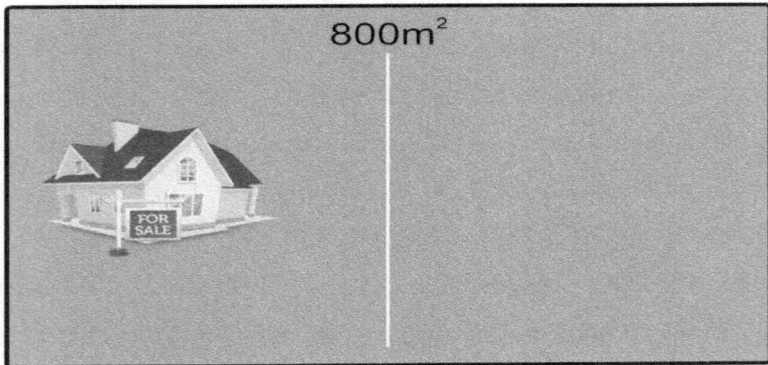

Figure 8.6: Property of a site

Source: Author

The main advantage of subdivision is that you can get a free block of land. Imagine you find a property with a large, long garden in the backyard? This tells you the site has potential for subdivision.

Say, for example, you found this property that has a land size of 800m². The property is flat land. Then you check with the local council that it complies with the zoning requirement, the width and the overall area. The next step is to subdivide it. Once subdivided, you are left with many options like holding the land for appreciation, building a property on it to increase the value for both properties, or sell it to make a profit and pay down your existing debt.

Figure 8.7: Potential for subdivision

Source: RP Data

The truth is that not many people can see this type of opportunity in front of their eyes. Even though these opportunities are in the same suburb they live in, and they walk past it day after day, year after year, they never see it. That is why I sometimes think that it's not money that holds people back from doing this type of deal. It is the lack of drive, knowledge and experience.

[Note: In Australia, minor subdivision starts at around $50,000. The main costs are development application costs, construction costs, infrastructure contributions and plan sealing charges. The exact details of each requirement of subdivision are easily accessible via each council's town planning scheme, most of which can be viewed online.]

Splitter

A splitter block is a term used to describe a large block that has already been split into two lots or subdivided. Often, there is a property already sitting there in the middle of the block. For example, lot 58 and 56 in the figure below are two different lots with a common property there. This is the same as lot 54 and 52, as well as lot 50 and lot 48.

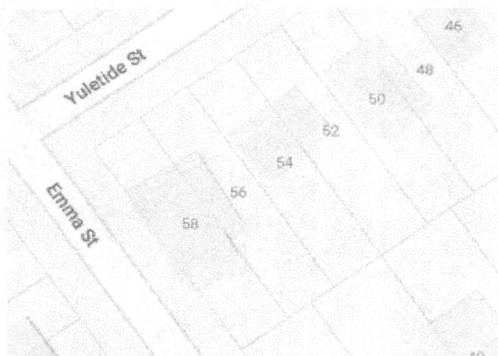

Figure 8.8: Potential for Splitter

Source: Author

In a splitter block deal, the strategy is to purchase the property in the two lots, demolish it and sell the two lots for a profit. However, before you do a splitter, you need to do your own due diligence and feasibility assessment. Always check with the local council about the regulation because some properties are subject to heritage control and cannot be demolished.

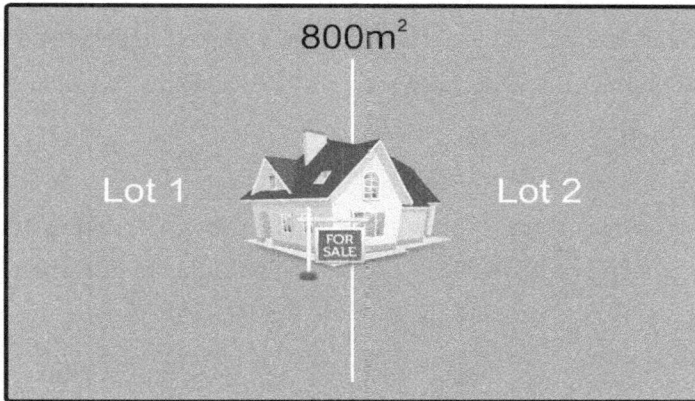

Figure 8.9: Property on a site

Source: Author

No Money Down

Here is a strategy that allows you to buy property with little or none of your own money. The good thing about a no money down deal is that it saves years of saving up for the deposit. The down side is that not all banks will allow this type of deal because of the valuation process, especially the major banks.

Traditionally, when you buy a property, say for $500,000, you will need a $100,000 deposit and stamp duty of $18,000, and then take out a $400,000 mortgage with the bank. This is a loan to value ratio LVR of 80%.

Assume you have difficulties saving up for the 20% deposit, the bank would allow you to take out lender mortgage insurance so that you can borrow up to 90% or at most 95%. For a 95% loan, this means that you are borrowing $475,000, and only need $43,000 (i.e. $25000 + $18,000) to enter the market!

Now, to execute a no money down deal successfully, you have to buy properties below market value. Instead of buying the property at the asking price of $500,000, negotiate it down to say, $450,000.

If you can do this, you are effectively buying the property with none of your own money, covering both the deposit and stamp duty, and enter the property market right away!

Does this make sense to you?

As good as this strategy might sound, major banks do not allow you to do this. They process your loan application based on their own valuation. However, some small banks or non-bank lenders allow you to use your own valuation.

But why are smaller banks doing this?

They do this to compete with major banks to get a deal from you. So, talk with your banker about using this strategy. Do your own research. You will get discouraged along the way. But keep trying. Think creatively.

Negative Gearing

Negative gearing is properly the most famous property strategy used by many property investors in Australia. It means buying property that has rental income less than the expense and the mortgage repayment. People buy negative gearing real estate for tax benefit. How negative gearing properties work is that the loss accumulated can be used to offset your income tax bracket.

The majority of property nowadays turns out to be negatively geared because of rising property prices. So, investors who buy negative geared property are most likely chasing after the capital gain.

In my opinion, buying negative geared property is against wealth principles and money rules.

Capital growth is not a certain thing. It can go up and down, depending on your suburb.

If you are chasing after negative gearing property to be financially free, you might be disappointed.

Even so, whichever strategy you use comes down to how you chart your course to financial freedom in your big picture. For example, you might have a plan to buy a negative geared property in an appreciating market, wait for a few years and sell it to pay down the debt for other properties to make them positive cashflow. There is no rule against this as long as you have a plan.

***

When assembling your real estate investing plan, you might want to combine one or more of these property strategies to form your own property investing strategy. The sky is your limit. But the most important thing is that you must take action. If you are young, and the deposit is your barrier against entering the property market, I strongly encourage you to use these strategies. Don't wait. Time is on your side.

Chapter 9

Hidden Secrets of Commercial Real Estate

As good as residential real estate may sound, it is only the tip of the iceberg on the subject of real estate investing. Before you get into residential real estate, it is best to know about commercial real estate as well.

Many people who have made it *really* big in real estate made it through commercial real estate. The figures I am talking about are $100 million or more. This type of goal is unlikely achievable through residential real estate. Real estate magnates, like the U.S. president, *Donald Trump*, achieve that goal in commercial real estate.

So, what is the difference between commercial real estate and residential real estate? Don't the tricks behind commercial real estate investing work just like residential real estate investing, except the dollar is much larger?

Commercial Real Estate vs. Residential Real Estates

Residential real estate is where people live. Commercial real estate is where people do business. Residential real estate is about people. Commercial real estate is about contracts.

They are different in many ways.

Say, for example, a tenant in a residential property has blocked the toilet, or a faucet is leaking. As the landlord, you will have to either pay someone to fix it or help the tenant to fix it yourself. Fixing it requires that you either make a schedule with a handyman or schedule your own time. Imagine if you have a bad tenant that gives you this kind of issue every month, this can be a real headache. In residential property, you have to specify that the rent needs to be paid on time, but the residential tenancy agreement is biased towards tenants most of the time. You can only evict a tenant for not paying rent if the rent is over 90 days late. Commercial real estate, on the other hand, has a more favourable contract to the landlord. In most commercial contracts, if the tenant does not pay rent on time, you have the right to enter the property and seize all business operations, sell their capital and charge a late fee. If the tenant does not pay the rent, there will be a penalty payment of x%, and it will start to accrue interest on a daily basis. Because the commercial real estate tenants tend to earn an income in the premises, they have a vast interest in looking after your premises for you.

Apart from that, in residential real estate, the tenant only pays the rent. So, the maintenance of real estate is the responsibility of the owner. For commercial real estate, the tenant pays for your outgoings. Commercial property uses a special type of lease called *triple net lease*, which means the tenant will pay property taxes, insurance and maintenance, in addition to the rent and utilities they pay to occupy the premises.

In addition, in residential real estate, the duration of the lease is relatively short, usually lasting for 6 months to 1 year. So, when the lease expires, you will have to look for another tenant. For commercial real estate, the lease is usually 5 years to 10 years. Some commercial leases can be as long as 25 years.

Best of all, commercial real estate can give you a significant larger cash flow. Commercial real estate rent never goes down but up. Every year, you can have annual increase in rent.

But, if commercial real estate is so good, why aren't many people going that already?

There are two disadvantages to commercial real estate that keep people from entry. Firstly, it is expensive and requires a much larger down payment. Banks will lend at most 70% of the value of the property. Secondly, it can be very difficult to find a tenant for commercial premises. But, it is exactly these two disadvantages that keep most people away from the investment of the rich. So, what if I say I can help you to overcome these challenges? In reality, commercial real estate investing is the ultimate test to your understanding of OPM, OPR, OPT and debts.

Capitalization Rate

If you remember, in a previous chapter, I talked about the concept of ROI.

$$ROI = \frac{Annual\ Profit}{Cost\ of\ Investment}$$

The ROI of residential real estate depends on many factors like the down payment, your rent, the expense, etc. In a nutshell, the ROI depends on the market.

Commercial property is an entirely different beast. For commercial property, you want to understand this formula:

$$Property\ Value = \frac{Rental\ Income}{Capitalization\ Rate}$$

But what does the capitalization rate (*Cap rate*) mean?

A cap rate is the rate at which you capitalize the income of a commercial property to arrive at the property value.

Let me give you an example. Let's say commercial property A has the potential to generate a rental income of $1,000,000 per year, with a *cap rate* of 10%. What this means is that when an investor buys this $1 million property, he expects to see a 10% return. To do so, he is willing to pay $10 million. This $10 million is the property value.

So, what determines the cap rate of a commercial property?

By definition, the average return of *similar buildings that have been sold* in the recent past determines the cap rate.

The rent, on the other hand, is not determined by the market but limited by your creativity. I will explain why with examples later.

So, there are two ways to increase the value of a commercial value. The first way is to increase the rent. If you are creative enough to double the rent, you double the property value. The second way to increase the value of a commercial value is a reduction in the *market cap rate*. *Cap rate* varies all the time. It falls in a strong market because investors accept a lower return in a strong market and rises in a weak market when investors are expecting a higher return to compensate for the risk.

So, assume you bought this commercial building for $1,000,000, which has a cap rate of 10% and generates a rental income of $100,000 annually. If the economy is good, and other similar commercial properties around you are doing well, the cap rate will reduce to say, 8%, and your property will be worth $1,250,000. On the other hand, if the economy is bad, and a recession hits, the cap rate will rise to 15%. In this case, the property will only be worth $666,666.

If you understand *cap rate*, then congratulations, you are on your way to making millions in commercial real estate.

When a commercial real estate agent advertises their property, they tend to phrase it in a way like: *the commercial property is selling at a cap rate of 12%*. To me, this is misleading. Phrasing it this way means they are dividing the rental income of the commercial property by *their asking price*. This has little meaning because until you find out about the market cap rate of similar commercial buildings, you'll never know the real *cap rate*. A commercial property could be selling a commercial at a cap rate of 12%, but the *market cap rate* is only 10%. In this case, you are buying below market value. However, the opposite is also true. So, instead of using cap rate, the real estate agents should be using ROI.

Types of Commercial Real Estate

Before you get started in commercial real estate, it is best to understand the different sectors of commercial real estate out there.

Commercial real estate can be categorised into three broad sectors.

1.   Industrial
2.   Office
3.   Retail

Industrial properties can be a warehouse, factories and workshops, etc. Typically, they have a higher yield than office and retail. Because industrial properties are usually rented by engineering companies or logistic companies, they generally provide higher yield as well as a longer lease. In addition, because businesses that rent industrial properties are usually of similar nature, any improvement made can be retained and used to negotiate for a higher rent when you re-lease it. Even so, industrial properties are not without drawbacks. It costs more money to maintain if it is vacant. Typically, it has lower capital growth compared to commercial properties in other sectors.

Figure 9.1: Warehouse

Source: realcommercial.com.au

Office spaces are commercial properties found in business parks and CBD office towers. They usually have a kitchen, meeting rooms and desk spaces. Typically, the tenants of office spaces are businesses like finance, insurance and administration. The best tenants are the government, banks and blue chip tenants. The yield of office space varies widely, depending on the location. However, office spaces are very sensitive to demand and supply. In places like the CBD, where there are a lot of supplies, most likely, the landlord will have to reduce the rent to stay competitive.

Figure 9.2: Office Space

Source: realcommercial.com.au

Retail properties are properties that sell goods and service like clothing, restaurants, bars, fashion stores, gyms, supermarkets, pharmacies, bakeries, shopping centres, etc. Typically, retail properties offer the lowest yield. They are very sensitive to the economy. During economic downturn, retail properties have a risk of vacancy. So, that is why it is very important to find out more about your tenant before signing the lease. Like office space, the location of retail properties is crucial. It is best to invest in a place where there is high traffic, as businesses depend on foot traffic to make income.

Figure 9.3: Retail

Source: realcommercial.com.au

Commercial Real Estate Cycle

Commercial real estate cycles are like traffic lights. When you spot a green light, it is buy time. Conversely, when it is red, you stop and wait.

The demand for commercial real estate is driven by economic conditions, which can be broken down into the health of the economy, unemployment rate, demographic, population growth, business confidence and interest rates. Since there are so many different sectors in commercial real estate, and each sector has its own driver of growth, you have to understand the market cycle of that specific sector you want to invest in as well as the area you want to buy. Never use the market cycle of office space and apply that to an industrial warehouse. Always compare apples with apples of the same type of commercial properties in the same neighbourhood or nearby zip codes.

All commercial real estate sectors will go through four phases:

*   Recovery
*   Expansion
*   Oversupply
*   Recession

These phases are based on the demand and supply of the commercial properties and occupancy.

The best time to buy is the Recovery Phase. During the recovery phase, there will be no new construction happening, and the vacancy rate will decline.

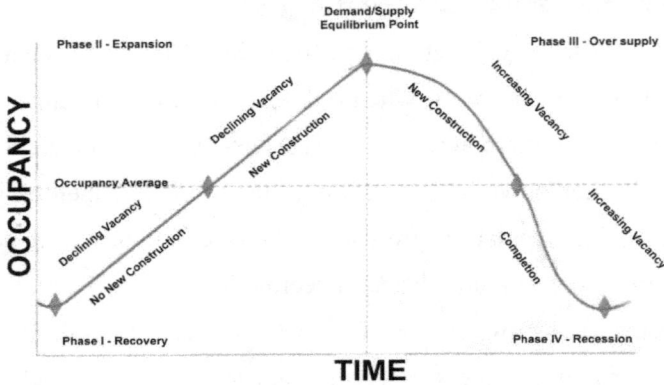

Figure 9.4: Market cycle of commercial real estate

Source: Author

As the economy expands, more new construction will happen, and more business will occupy commercial real estate until the market reaches equilibrium. As more and more supply of commercial properties enters the market, there will be an oversupply at some point, and the vacancy rate will rise. When the recession hits, it is the worst time to enter the market because there will be a lot of vacancies, and it is very hard to find a tenant.

Guide to Investing in Commercial Real Estate

Investing in commercial real estate is a fast track to financial freedom. First, it has higher yield and better cashflow. Second, you can grow your equity very quickly. Basically, investing in commercial property is a mix of cashflow and capital gain strategy.

But to ripe the benefit of commercial real estate, you must buy correctly step by step.

Below are the steps you must follow to buy commercial properties.

1.   Find a commercial property

2.   Due Diligence

3.   Negotiating a deal

4.   Financing

5.   Structuring the Lease

6.   Tenants

7.   Add Value

STAGE ONE: FIND A COMMERCIAL PROPERTY

The first step is to know what to look for and where to look.

When you start looking for a commercial property, the best starting point is *location, location, and location*. The location you pick must be a busy area. Avoid quiet streets or ghost towns. Business people do their own diligence and will only rent places where there is a lot of potential customers. So, investing in a commercial property in a high traffic area means you will have a low vacancy rate to start off. Talk to the locals and get a feel for the suburb. Get a look at the police report about the area. Always remember, it is the location first. You can always modify the building but not the neighbourhoods.

Next, you want to find out the commercial real estate cycle of the type of property you invest in and the specific location you want to buy.

You can find commercial property in many ways: newspaper, the Internet, networking, commercial real estate firms, etc. Once you have found a commercial property with potential, you have to do your due diligence by looking at the numbers.

STAGE TWO: DUE DILIGENCE

Do you know the Eiffel Tower, one of the most recognizable and well-trafficked monuments in the world, was sold twice by the same man because he did not do enough due diligence?

Figure 9.5: The Eiffel Tower

Source: Author

Like residential real estate, doing your due diligence means doing your homework. There are four major areas in the due diligence process in commercial real estate.

1.   Legal

2.   Technical

3.   Planning & Environment

4.   Financial

There is no way you are going to be an expert in all four areas. You need to leverage other people's experience (OPR) to do this.

Take legal, for example, commercial zoning laws control the type of activities a business may conduct in a particular area and the category of business that can occupy the zoned area. For example, your tenant might be operating a hamburger business in your premises. But a sudden change in zoning means he or she can no longer operate a food business. That is why, in this case, you need a solicitor on your team. They will check if your tenant might have a variance for an exemption to zoning law.

For technical due diligence, you will need building inspectors, a town planner, surveyors or engineers to check for information, such as maintenance contract review, fire engineering solutions, condition of the building structure, etc. This book will not cover every possible technical due diligence you need to check, so you need to talk with the experts.

Planning & Environment is also very important. It checks for current zoning requirements, the floor space ratio of a building, development approval, height restriction, potential environmental contamination issues, etc.

For finance, you need to work out the vacancy rate, the yield of the property and the cap rate, recent sales, rental comparison, the seller's need, the cashflow, the lease, how long has the property been on the market, why is the owner selling, the valuation, etc.

STAGE THREE: NEOTIGATE A DEAL

With commercial property, the price is based on the rental income divided by the cap rate. Since all sellers know their rental income, the only way to negotiate is about the recent sales cap rate. Negotiation on the cap rate is how you can buy a commercial property below market value.

For a successful negotiation, you need to present the problems you have found during your due diligence to the seller. You can also persuade them with your understanding of the market cycle of the commercial property sector.

The items that you want to negotiate with the seller include the following:

- Settlement time
- Rental Guarantee
- General Maintenance
- Building Maintenance

- Vendor Finance
- Subject to DA prior to settlement

If you recall the formula of commercial real estate, you will understand that a vacant property costs less than a tenanted one. So, a very powerful skillset of the commercial real estate investor is to be able to find tenants. Besides using traditional methods to look for tenants, you may also leverage freelance sites like Fiverr or Upwork. These sites will cost as little as $5 for someone to post flyers or cold call to help you find tenants. Most people hate the step of finding tenants because of uncertainties. But, like any business, finding tenants is governed by the Law of Average. You might spend $5 to post 100 flyers or $500 to post 10,000 flyers. But, the point is, you only need to find one tenant, and you are done.

If you become good at finding tenants, it is entirely possible to buy a vacant commercial property below market value and find a tenant before you even settle to make your property appreciate.

STAGE FOUR: FINANCING

The high cost of commercial real estate is one reason that pulls people away from commercial real estate. Assume you have found a commercial property; once you have worked out the numbers, the next thing you have to do is to finance it.

I talked about creative finance earlier in this chapter. You can always use techniques like vendor finance, joint ventures and a combination of other strategies to reduce your risk.

In terms of getting a loan for commercial property, if you opt for the traditional way of finance, anything below $1 million would require a 20% deposit. For anything higher than $1 million, you will need at least 30% deposit.

Also, unlike a residential property loan, a commercial property loan has a much shorter loan term, which is between 2 to 15 years, or 30 years if you use your residential securities. Either way, you will need a greater capacity for repayment. They will also require an annual review to access your profit and loss.

That is why you will always need to use a commercial loan broker. They can help you to waive the annual review and help you to get the right loan terms. Do not go for any broker or traditional big banks to take out a commercial loan. Go for an experienced commercial property broker, as they deal with smaller banks and other lenders that offer a longer loan term, a lower deposit and a longer interest only period.

A commercial loan is less strict compared with a residential loan. There are fewer legislative restrictions.

In commercial real estate, your experienced commercial property broker will offer you *No doc, low doc* loans that do not require proof of income. For example, the approval of a *Lease doc* loan is based on the income from the commercial lease rather than the investor's finance. In fact, for expensive commercial property, the bank will pretty much focus more on the potential performance of the commercial property than your financial situation. They will base their loan on the lease, not your income. That is why you need to present your information correctly. You want to show them the strength of your application for them to give you the money. You want to include the location of your security property, the team involved and their experience, the lease terms, the tenant's details and their financial capacity, the industry, your tenant, etc. The bank will look at all these factors for risk evaluation to decide your final interest rate.

[Note: You will have to do your own research and talk with the professionals when applying for a commercial property loan. This section is for reference only because the market changes from time to time.]

STAGE FIVE: STRUCTURING THE LEASE

At the beginning of this section, we talked about commercial real estate is about contract. So, a commercial lease is the most important element when investing in commercial real estate.

There are four types of lease in commercial real estate:

1.   Gross Lease – The owner is responsible for everything. The rent collected covers all the expenses in building and utilities, etc.

2.   Net Lease – The tenant pays for one or more of the building's utilities.

3.   Triple Net Lease – The owner is responsible for the building structure. Tenants pay the outgoing expenses.

4.   Absolute Triple Net Lease – The tenants pays for everything.

In a lease structure, you want to make sure that the rent your tenant is paying matches the rent for the size of the commercial property in that location.

Always seek professional advice to word your lease correctly. Check and make sure no confusing clause contradicts one another. You really need a solicitor to state the responsibility clearly. Don't be shy and always ask the solicitor questions if there are things you do not understand about the lease. Remember, there is no such question as a silly question.

STAGE SIX: TENANTS

A good lease structure and a good tenant are key to positive successful cashflow.

But how can you identify a good tenant?

Typically, government and blue chip companies are very good tenants.

But not all tenants are like this. That is why you need a checklist to define whether your tenant is good or not.

There are two key points to identifying a good tenant.

1.   The length of tenancy

2.   Payment history

3.   Correct rent for the size of the premise.

You want to know how long your potential tenant has been renting. You want to make sure tenants have a good record in payment history. Next, you want a long lease. A short lease contract in commercial real estate is a big no-no. You want a long lease because every year, you can raise the rent. In some instances, you want to structure your lease so that if you make any improvements to the property for their business purpose, you are going to increase the rent by x amount of dollars. This is a good option because by raising the rent, you are increasing the value of the property.

STAGE SEVEN: ADD VALUE

An increase in rent means an increase in property value. So, finding ways how to increase the rent will tremendously boost the value of a commercial property. To do this, you need creativity. You need to discover the hidden upside potential of your property that others do not see. Beside the cashflow, discovering hidden upsides after revaluation will increase the equity of your commercial property very quickly.

The best ways to find a hidden upside is to develop an instinct by looking at more commercial properties or have a commercial property consultant. Let me give you an example. If you have a large retail space, instead of renting it to one business, why not talk to the business owner to see if they want less space with a reduction in rent? This way, you can rent out other space to another business and get double rent. This arrangement will reduce your risk, boost your income, and increase the value of your property.

Apart from that, many companies would like to put their name on the premises. They will lose all rational thought and will negotiate all possible ways just to have their company name on the building. This is called *Naming Rights*. As the commercial property owner, you can charge higher rent just for *Naming Rights*. This is basically free cash and free equity.

So, you see, the skill to add value is limited only by your imagination. That is why, unlike a residential property, the value of a commercial property is limited only by the owner's creativity. An experienced commercial real estate investor will always question what he or she can do to find that hidden upside. They will always look for a win-win as to what can be done to help the business owner in exchange for an increase in rent. I came across a business owner in the electric motor industry, who was happy to pay an extra $450 a month in rent just to have a $1,500 web cam security system installed in the warehouse.

Every commercial property has some kind of hidden upside to it. And it is very important to find these upsides. Keep these upsides to yourself. You do not need to tell the real estate agent about them. Use them only to your advantage.

Using a LLC to Own Commercial Property

I hope you have a brief understanding of commercial property.

Besides the technical side of commercial real estate investing, I want to stress the importance of asset protection.

Setting up a limited liability company to own every commercial property you purchase is a step that cannot be ignored. In case an injury happens in your building, and the business decides to sue you, your entire investment portfolio could be exposed if your asset is not under the umbrella of an

LLC. However, if you set up an LLC correctly with your attorney to own your commercial properties, the business can only sue the LLC, not you or any of your assets.

The Art of the Deal

"I like thinking big. I always have. To me, it's very simple. If you're going to be thinking anyway, you might as well think big."

-Donald J. Trump.

Donald Trump, the 45th President of the U.S. and a real estate mogul, is the very definition of an American success story. His skyscrapers changed the face of the New York skyline. *Trump: The Art of the Deal* is an international bestseller I strongly recommend. It is a great read. Despite being written in the late 80s, the lessons inside have stood the test of time. From the building of the Trump Tower to the battle for Hilton, the book reveals Trump's secrets on how he built his real estate empire. It is more than just negotiation. It is now how you approach big problems in real estate and elevate yourself. It is a business book that every successful real estate investor should read.

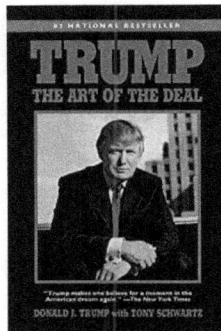

Figure 9.6: The Art of the Deal

Source: Donald Trump

Question and Answers

I know you will probably have a lot of questions on how to chart your path to financial freedom with real estate. Below are some of the most common questions real estate investors will ask, whether they are beginning to invest in real estate or building their real estate portfolio already. This Q&A section will save you a lot of time and help you to chart your course.

What Mistakes do People Make in Real Estate Investing?

Not investing is probably the number one mistake people make. People can read a lot of information, go to a lot of seminars, and read a lot of books like this one. But, in the end, they take no action. Inaction is the worst thing you can do in real estate investing, so don't be one of them.

The second mistake people make is waiting too long. They time the market, waiting for a correction. As I have pointed out with the property cycle, you are forgoing a lot of opportunities if you decide to wait for a crash. Banks are very strict on their lending policy during a correction phase. That is why the best way is to jump into the market once you have saved up.

The third mistake people make is to think they know it all already. There is no one who knows it all. The market changes all the time. Tax laws will change. The smart way is to open up for new ideas and keep learning.

The last mistake property investors make is by being too emotional. They buy properties based on emotions, not on numbers.

How to Build a Property Portfolio to become financially free?

Most people invest in properties just for the purpose of investing in properties. They never have a plan to become financially independent. So, in the end, they will end up nowhere like a jellyfish.

So, that is why your goal is to go outside your comfort zone to build a property portfolio with 10+ properties to become financially free in a short time frame. You do not want to buy one or two properties, pay off the debt in the next 30 years, and retire.

To begin, you should always buy properties below market value. The property you aim for should be neutral or slightly negative property with a lot of growth potential. It should not be an expensive property. The price range you should be looking for is around $300,000 to $400,000.

Say, for example, in the first year, property A is listed for $400,000. Always negotiate the price down below market value to $350,000. Continue to save.

In the second year, go to the bank for revaluation of property A. Since you bought property A below market value, you will have at least $50,000 equity. Refinance to extract the equity out. With some extra saving, you can use this as a deposit for property B. This property should be listed for $400,000 in another suburb with high growth potential. Again, negotiate the price down below market value.

So, in the third year, you have property A and property B. Go to the bank, refinance to extract the extra equity out. Use the equity as a deposit for property C, which should also be $400,000 in a higher growth area. Again, negotiate the price down and repeat the process.

By the end of the decade, you will have ten properties with high growth under your belt. The initial negative cashflow properties will turn positive. You can choose to sell four properties and pay down the debt of the other six you have. The sky is your limit.

Of course, this is an overly simplified example to build a property portfolio. But the point is that the faster you can execute these steps, the harder your equity works for you, the faster you will become financially independent.

Cashflow vs. Capital Gain

When you begin, you might be struggling with what type of property strategy you should go for. Should you invest for capital gain or cash flow?

I think you should invest in both.

If you invest in the positive cashflow property first, the property will most likely be in regional areas or student accommodation like a studio. These properties will have low growth potential. If you invest in these properties, you might be collecting a low net income only.

If you invest in negative cashflow property first, it will reduce your standard of living. The more negative cashflow properties you accumulate, the less likely the bank is going to lend you to buy more properties. Eventually, you will max out your borrowing capacity and will not be able to buy any more properties.

The best type of property is the one that is neutral or slightly negative cashflow with high growth potential. These properties allow you to build a property portfolio that eventually replaces your income. You can enjoy the capital gain to extract that extra equity out and use it as a deposit to buy the next property. Over time, your negative cashflow properties will turn positive. I believe this strategy can give you the most options in this new economy.

Chart Your Financial Journey

Congratulations if you've made it this far in the book.

By now, I hope you have a comprehensive knowledge on the subject of investing in real estate. From time to time, you might want to revisit some of the techniques used. Don't be afraid to experiment with these real estate tricks, combine them, and tailor them to your own financial circumstances.

I hope I have done a good job revealing some of the hidden secrets in investing in real estate.

Now, it is time for you to take action.

Chapter 10

Hidden Secrets of Property Development

Contrary to conventional belief, I think that just anybody can get into property development. It doesn't matter what age you are, what your background is, how much money you have or don't have. None of that actually matters. The only thing that matters is that you have a passion in property development, have the knowledge and actually do it.

There are two types of property investors: passive property investors and active property investors. Passive property investors wait for equity to rise. They buy and hold it for years. Active property investors actively create equity. They always ask themselves what they can do to increase the value of the property and make money now. And this is what property development is about.

Again, it is not that one type of property investor is better than the other. They both have pros and cons. But the truth is, active property investors create wealth *faster* than passive property investors. If you'd rather wait 10 to 20 years to see the result of property, then passive property investing is for you. However, if you want to see the result in investing in property within weeks or months, then you probably want to look into active property investing.

This section is about the basic knowledge of property development. In this section, you will learn about the use of knowledge and skills of a developer to assemble profitable property deals. You will also learn about the seven stages of property development and how to do a feasibility assessment.

Everything Has a Product Cycle

Every product we use in our society, whether it is T-shirts, drinks, electronics, makeup, all go through a product cycle. It works like this. First, it starts with inventors who have an idea about a product. They invent the prototype. The factory manufactures the product and sells it to wholesalers. The wholesalers package the product and give it to retailers in the shops. The retailers sell the product to people on the street. At every single stage of this product cycle, someone is making money, except for the person buying the product on the street.

Property, like any other product, has the same product cycle.

For people buying real estate, waiting for it to appreciate, he or she is the person on the street paying at the very end of the product cycle. Most people get involved in property by paying the money to buy property at a retail price. They are not making money out of the product cycle of property as an insider.

Let me give you an example. Have you been to 7-Eleven and seen how expensive a can of Coca-Cola cost? Once, I saw one in 7-Eleven selling at $4 per can. And a couple of blocks away in Costco, I saw them selling at a far cheaper price, like $2 per can, a 50% discount. I am sure Costco is making money by selling it for $2 a can. But my point is, is 50% per can of Coca-Cola a great deal already?

The truth is, we don't know.

The reason is that we don't know the product cycle of Coca-Cola. We do not know how much more margins there are in the supply chain. For some products, the margin in the product cycle can be as high as 200% to 300%.

So, that is why you need to understand the product cycle of a property in order to create a profitable deal. You need to know the pricing from the beginning of a product cycle. In property development, the product developer is the supplier of the property cycle. In order to get the best deal, you need to speak their language and understand property from the eye of a product developer.

So, I hope you understand that when people traditionally buy property, they are buying at the very last stage of the property cycle. You, on the other hand, want to deal directly with the developer to get the best deal.

But to do so, you need to speak their language. You need to understand the *stuff*.

You need to understand the product cycle of property development because it sets the price of property. If you don't, you will be paying the retail price.

The Seven Stages of Property Development

I remember when I was just a kid in Hong Kong, every day in the morning, I would see construction sites on my way to school by bus. To me, I had the impression that property development is all about construction. Today, I realize that back then, I was not looking at the entire picture at all.

People always tend to think that development is always about construction. This is not true. In fact, construction is stage six of the seven-stage property development cycle. A lot of money was made way before construction happened.

To make money in property development, you want to become the dealmaker in the seven stages of the property development cycle. You will find an opportunity and connect someone to that opportunity. Don't restrict yourself to the idea that the only way in property development is to build something and sell.

To become a property dealmaker, you need to understand the seven stages of property development.

STAGE ONE: FIND A SITE
The first stage of property development is to find a site. A site doesn't only mean raw land. It can be land with a property already on it that you see has potential for development.

When executing the first step, you want to skip finding it on big Internet sites or newspapers. This is where you buy a $4 can of Coca-Cola in 7-Eleven. The sites you should be finding are usually off market. They are sold by development agents off market.

In Australia, in the Sydney Morning Herald, development agents advertise in the Business Weekend in the commercial and industrial section. In your country, there should be similar advertisements. Start picking up your phone and calling these people. The advertisement will be like a small listing with tiny words:

DEVELOPMENT SITE WANTED

What you want to do is to call these people and tell them you are a property developer and ask them to put you on their contact list if they find any deals.

In fact, have you ever wondered why in some sites, some development is happening but was never advertised it was for sale?

A lot of these development sites were sold by development agents before they even hit the market.

This is exactly how the inside industry works. You need to connect to the right people. That is why you need to be on the list of development agents. Once you are on their list, they will email out these off market deals to you.

Another great resource in finding a site is from the council. You can get maps and council plans from the council website for free. There are two documents you need to look at: The *environmental plan* and the *zoning map*. These two documents tell you what you can and cannot build in an area. If land is zoned for low-density residential only, you cannot build medium density residential. If land is zoned for commercial core, it can only be used to build commercial property. If a property in a zone is heritage, you cannot knock it down and rebuild at all.

Figure 10.1: Hurstville Local Environmental Plan 2014

Source: St George Council

So, by going through their environmental plan, zoning map, doing a feasibility assessment of the site and calling the developer agent daily, you are actually doing your homework in stage one.

If you find a profitable deal and you present well to a developer, they will pay you what the industry calls a *Site finder fee*. In other words, you do not need to own the site. All you need to know is how to find a profitable development site that a developer wants to develop.

But why would a developer pay you in advance for a property you don't even own?

The truth is that a developer does not have the time to look for a deal. He is too busy working on existing deals. For developers, time is money. They want to finish the existing one and go right to the next project.

When you are driving around next time, go to places that already have construction happening. This means that there are probably development opportunities around there. If you see a street where half of the properties are units and the other half are old houses, and you check the zoning map to see they are medium density residential, the chances are these houses have development potential to be medium density residential. Go and door knock these house owners and see if they are potential sellers. If they are, congratulations, you have just become a property dealmaker between developers and sellers. A *Site finder fee* could range between $15,000 to $35,000 or higher, depending on the scale of the development.

STAGE TWO: SITE ANALYSIS

The second stage of the seven stages of property development is site analysis. In this stage, you have to do careful research to decide if you are going ahead with the property development deal. During site analysis, you have to look at the market, the existing comparative developments on the market, the potential for the land to develop a property, and many other factors as well.

When you look at the market, you want to look at what you are going to build on this site that will attract buyers in that area. Understand who lives in this area and who wants to live in this area you are developing.

The good news is that most of this information you research is free. You can call real estate agents and ask them what types of properties are hot selling. Is it a townhouse, villa, duplex, units or apartment? Understand the demographics of an area by looking at government statistic websites and local council websites. At the end of the day, it is the council's job to build a suburb that is the best result for that area. They spend a lot of money on research, and you can get the data for free. If you approach a town planner, they will give you excellent advice on what to build in that area in terms of profitability.

STAGE THREE: FEASIBILITY

The third stage is feasibility. And feasibility is all about profits. Never ever buy a property until you have done your research, your site analysis and feasibility. The most important thing in feasibility is to have accurate figures. That is why you need software specific for property development.

A professional feasibility calculator will help you to work out all the associated costs in property development. It will give you a profit in percentage and dollars. In property development, you need at least 20% profit to have any worthwhile property development deal. Do not merely look at the dollars on how much you make. You need to look at the **percentage in profit**. Besides, 20% is what banks need to look at when they assess your feasibility analysis for finance. It is the minimum you need for the margin of error.

But how can you increase the profit percentage to be more than 20%?

The way to do so is to maximize land usage.

There are so many potential things you can build on a block of land. Picture what you can build on it. Maybe some of you are thinking of building townhouses. Maybe you are thinking of building units. Work with your architects, and he/she will work out the land size based on the council guidelines to make sure that you can get as much out of the land usage as possible.

Figure 10.2: Block of land

Source: Author

STAGE FOUR: FINANCING

The fourth stage of property development is about financing. Instead of getting a conventional loan, ask the bank for a commercial loan.

Property development is a commercial activity. However, unlike other businesses where you can have cashflow, a property developer will only get their profits after they have completed the deal.

But, how would the bank charge the developer interest in a commercial loan?

Here is what happens: The bank will add up all the interest every single month. The developer does not have to pay it back until the end of the development. It is called *capitalized finance*. The loan is structured in a way that the developer owner does not have to pay the interest back until they've made a profit.

If it weren't for *capitalized finance*, a lot of development you see wouldn't be happening today. But the downside for *capitalized finance* is that the bank will charge a higher interest rate.

For a typical commercial loan in property development, the bank will lend you 50% to 70% of the property value. So, for a $1,000,000 development project, the bank will lend you 70%, but you still need to come up with 30%, which is $300,000.

Unlike traditional real estate developers, developers do not save for the deposit. To come up with the $300,000 deposit, developers often use creative finance by applying OPM rules. One of the common ways is vendor finance. For example, you are planning to build a block of units on a site that has a house on it. You negotiate with the owner to finance your deposit and give them one of the units at the end of development for free on top of the price of the house he sold. This is a win-win. Sometimes, the vendor might be willing to vendor finance you more than you may require for a deposit. You may want to get a broker to help you to do a No Money Down deal like this for development. But you don't want to get just any broker. Many brokers only have knowledge on how to do a traditional residential property deal. To do a development deal, you will need a broker who can speak the language of creative finance and present your ideas properly to get the loan from the bank with the vendor finance deposit.

STAGE FIVE: DEVELOPMENT APPROVAL

The fifth stage of property development is development approval.

In reality, the more uses you can create on a property, the higher the value a DA will be. A block of ten units provides more value compared to a house on the same piece of land. But, before you create that value, you need to get your development plan approved.

Development approval is basically a plan you submit to the council about the plan of a specific property you want to build. And if the council approves, you are allowed to proceed to build.

Once you have a DA of a site, the value of the property goes up. It went up because you have increased the use of the property, thus its potential.

Up to this stage, we have not even built anything. All you did is to get a piece of paper approved to increase the value of the property. In the previous section, I talked about how you can use options to hold a property, get a DA, and then sell it to a developer for a profit. That developer will be your potential buyer. He is looking for property that already has a DA in place. He doesn't have time to wait for a DA to be done. Time is a cost to him. So, as soon as he finishes his current project, he wants to jump right onto the next one.

DA is one way to make money in the property development cycle without even buying the property, getting a loan or paying interest.

STAGE SIX: CONSTRUCTION

The sixth stage of property development is construction. You, as the developer or real estate dealmaker, will not actually build the property brick by brick. Your job is just to assemble profitable property deals. Below is an organisational chart of what property development looks like. As you have more projects, you will need a project manager to help you to communicate with the builder, who will then coordinate with the site manager and tradesmen. This is what makes development possible.

Property Developer
⬇
Project Manager
⬇
Builder
⬇
Site Manager
⬇
Tradesmen

Figure 10.3: Organisational Chart of Property Development

Source: Author

STAGE SEVEN: SELLING

Selling is the last stage of the property development cycle. The best technique a property developer can use is to sell property *off the plan*. You don't want to wait until the entire construction is complete before you start to sell. It takes too long.

But to sell off the plan, you need good architects to present your vision to the public. You have to use an artist's impression to have your final product look presentable and appealing.

***

I hope by now that you have a good understand of the seven stages of property development.

Can you see that you can get into property investing, even if you do not have any money? Do you see how you can make money through property without even buying property?

You do not need a deposit to get into property. Please get rid of this concept.

Instead of saving up year after year, a better alternative would be to understand the seven stages of property development and be a deal maker.

Please note that you don't need to do all seven stages to make money. But you have to understand them so that you can see profitable deals, and connect people to make a profit.

At the end of the day, get started no matter what age you are. Taking action is the key. Success is based on 70% psychology, 20% knowledge and 10% skills. This book is just about this 20%.

Don't wonder. Take action.

Chapter 11

Hidden Secrets of Stocks

There is a saying that the bull goes up by the stairs, and the bear goes out the window. History shows that money can be made much faster in a bear market than a bull market. I cannot agree more.

I have been through at least three bear markets in my life: The Asian Financial Crisis of 1997, the subprime mortgage crisis of 2008 and the coronavirus crisis of 2020. Experience taught me that people who buy and hold in the stock market are more than likely to lose in the long-term. It is entirely possible for someone to invest in the stock market for their entire life and lose it all just before they are about to retire. Worst of all, our retirement accounts, like a 401K or superannuation, are being invested by companies in the name of helping people to save up for their retirement. We all know what happened to our retirement account when the coronavirus crisis hit in the first half of 2020. They have no control over the investment. They are all at the mercy of how the market moves.

That is why I am not a big advocate for investing in stock. Investing in paper assets is a zero sum game. It is not a path to true wealth. Unless you are an insider who knows news before the rest of the market, you are more likely to lose in the long-term.

Even so, it is good to understand the basics of all types of investment. Stocks are very liquid and have an easy entry level. Stocks that pay dividends can also provide positive cash flow. The main reason I include this chapter is that I want to share some techniques with you in investing in paper assets. These techniques are not just useful for stocks but for investing in other asset classes as well.

This chapter is divided into four parts:

1.   Fundamental Analysis (Information)
2.   Technical Analysis (Information)
3.   Stock Investing Strategies (Positioning)
4.   Hedging (Positioning)

If you boil down stock investing into its essence, it is all about getting the information and positioning yourself to make a profit. There are two ways to get information: fundamental analysis and technical analysis.

Fundamental analysis is about understanding numbers in financial statements, which tells you the financial health of a company. Technical Analysis is about being able to read charts, which tells you the demand and supply of a company's stock. However, in reality, financial statements may lie. If you heard of the bankruptcy of Enron in 2001, you would probably know what I mean. Companies can use financial tricks to camouflage their loss or gain; however, they cannot lie about what the market thinks. That is why you need to understand both fundamental analysis and technical analysis to get the full picture.

Once you master fundamental and technical analysis, you will learn how to turn this information into your position to make a profit. Since we do not have a crystal ball, we do not have 100% certainty on which way the market goes. So, our positions will depend on what strategy we use and how to hedge the risk against any sudden change in the market.

By understanding and applying these four main areas in stock investing, you are increasing your probability of beating the average in investing in stocks.

How Does the Stock Market Work?

The stock market is made up of a vast ocean of investors who buy and sell stocks. If there are more buyers than sellers, the price of a stock goes up. And if the opposite happens, the price of a stock goes down.

When we purchase stock, we do not deal directly with the sellers. We buy through someone called the *market maker*. A *market maker* is specialist who makes the liquidity of the stock market possible.

Suppose you have 10 shares of Apple (NASDAQ: AAPL), and you want to sell them? How do you know there will be buyers who wants that exact 10 shares?

Here is how it works. Let's say, Peter wants to buy AAPL with a list price of $316.73 USD per share. This price is called the *ask price*, which is the price the *market maker* is willing to sell. Suppose Peter wants to sell the same stock? The market maker will buy it back for $316.78 USD per share. This price is called the *bid price*. Do you notice there is a $0.08 USD difference? This is called the *spread*. This is how the *market maker* makes a living. The more transactions made, the more money *market makers* made.

Since *market makers* buy and sell stock every second, if a stock price becomes too high or too low, they need to adjust it; otherwise, the number of transactions will slow down. To do so, they must keep a balance between buying and selling by raising or lowering the price based on the demand and supply of the stock.

As you have probably realized, a *market maker* doesn't care about the price of stock; all they need is to ensure an equilibrium between buyers and sellers so that there are always transactions happening.

What moves share price?

Contrary to conventional thinking, the price of a stock does not always go with the earnings of a company. What drives a stock price higher is the demand and supply of shares. It is the actual buying of stock that pushes its price higher.

The fundamentals of a company are only one factor influencing the price of stock. There can be other factors, such as rumour and news, or many other reasons that affect it as well.

That is why you need to know both fundamental analysis and technical analysis to get as much information as possible about the stock you buy.

Financial Jargons in the Stock Market

Before you invest in stock, there is some financial jargon you need to know. Knowing this financial jargon will make investing in stock more meaningful for you. Below is the key data of AAPL. There is a lot of information in this table about the stock. Let's start off with market capitalization.

Exchange	NASDAQ-GS	Market Cap	1,372,813,924,550
Sector	Technology	P/E Ratio	24.84
Industry	Computer Manufacturing	Forward P/E 1 Yr.	25.73
1 Year Target	$325.00	Earnings Per Share(EPS)	$12.75
Today's High/Low	$324.24/$316.50	Annualized Dividend	$3.28
Share Volume	31,367,004	Ex Dividend Date	May 8, 2020
AverageVolumeLabel	45,147,551	Dividend Pay Date	May 14, 2020
Previous Close	$318.89	Current Yield	1.03%

Figure 11.1: AAPL key data

Source: NASDAQ

Market Capitalization

Market capitalization is the market value of all the stocks. For example, if ABC Pty Ltd has 10,000 shares, and each share is $10, the market capitalization is $100,000.

Market capitalization = Number of shares x Price of share

AAPL has a market cap of $1.37 trillion. If we used the previous closing price of $318.89, it means that there is about 4 billion issued and outstanding shares.

[Note: Issued shares are the shares of the company that are issued by the company and held by its shareholders and investors. Outstanding shares are Issued shares minus the stock in treasury.]

A small company with a small market cap tends to be more risky. The good side is that it has more growth potential compared to companies with a big market cap like Apple.

Share Volume

Share volume is the number of shares that actually trade hands in a given day. Each transaction contributes to the volume. The more volume, the more liquid is a stock.

P/E Ratio

P/E ratio is the price to earnings ratio of a stock. The price in here is what investors are willing to pay for a stock. The earning is how much money a company makes.

PEG (Price, Earning, Growth)

Besides price and earnings, growth is the third factor that investors look at when they invest in stock. PEG gives information to investors about the growth of the company's earnings.

52 Weeks High/Low

A 52-week high is the highest share price that a stock has traded during a passing year.

Fundamental Analysis

Every entity has a financial statement. Whether it is a person, a company or even a country, a financial statement of an entity shows you their financial strength. Fundamental analysis is the evaluation of the financial statement of a company. It is like an X-ray of a company. It tells investors about the risks and value. By performing fundamental analysis, investors can make intelligence decisions on which stock to invest.

A financial statement of a company has two components: Income Statement and Balance Sheet. The *income statement* will tell you two things: Income (I) and Expenses (E). The net result is the *cashflow* of a business.

$$Cashflow = I - E$$

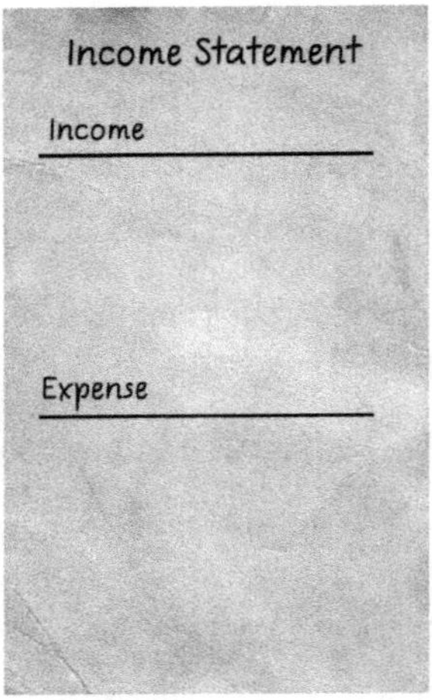

Figure 11.2: Income Statement

Source: Author

The balance sheet will have assets (A) and liability (L). Assets can be tangible assets like buildings equipment, machinery and business vehicles. They can also be intangible assets like intellectual property, trademark and databases. The liabilities of a company are like loans and account payable, etc. Equity is the difference between asset and liability.

$$Equity = A - L$$

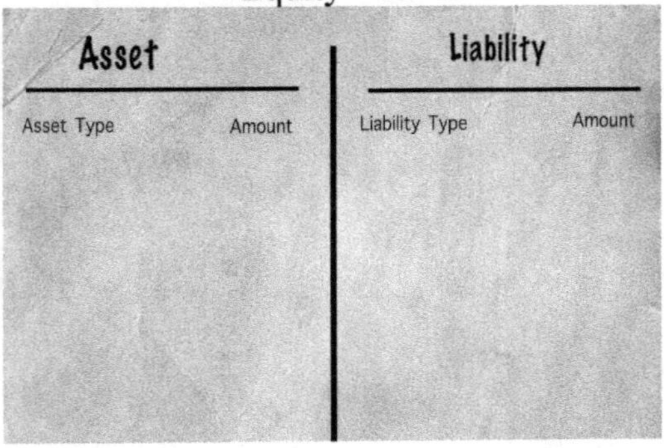

Figure 11.3: Balance Sheet

Source: Author

When doing fundamental analysis, you look at the income, expense, asset, liability, cashflow and equity of a company.

Let me give you an example. Below is a simplified financial statement of a fictional company – XYZ Pty Ltd. It is a company that makes vitamins. This year, XYZ Pty Ltd made $15 million in profit. It has $70 million in assets to make that income. However, these assets are only possible because of the $50 million borrowed money. Since XYZ Pty has an expense of $13 million due to paying rent and employees, its cashflow is $2 million.

XYZ Pty Ltd

Income
$15 Million
Expense
$13 Million

Assets	Liability
$70 Million	$50 Million

Figure 11.4: XYZ Pty Ltd Financial Statement

Source: Author

When doing fundamental analysis, it is always important to look at how much assets a company has and how much liability it had incurred. In this case, since XYZ Pty Ltd has assets much greater than its liability, it means it is using its debt wisely for growth.

Not all company liability is bad. So we can't just look at the size of a company's liability. In fact, if XYZ Pty Ltd decided to sell some assets to pay off its liability, it might not be able to generate $15 million.

Let's look at another example. Mask Pty Ltd is a mask manufacturing company. It has $5 million worth of assets to produce $1.1 million income. But because of the high interest repayment and high cost of renting factories, it is very expensive to make this profit. As you can see, Mask Pty Ltd is in a dire financial situation. It has negative equity of $2 million and is making a loss of $200,000 annually.

Mask Pty Ltd

Income
$1.1 Million
Expense
$1.3 Million

Assets	Liability
$5 Million	**$7 Million**

Figure 11.5: Mask Pty Ltd Financial Statement

Source: Author

Now, let's say that XYZ Pty Ltd has a share price of $300 per share, and Mask Pty Ltd's share price is $10 per share. Which one should you buy?

Average investors pick stocks based on price. They buy based on what is cheap or what news commentators say is good. Fundamental analysis, however, is about evaluating a company's stock based on its value, not the price. By understanding fundamental analysis, you will make better investment decisions when picking a stock.

But what is the valuation of a company?

Let me give you a simplified version.

Mike just started his Kettle Corn business in the middle of a busy shopping centre. This is what his income statement looks like. He has a cashflow or earnings of $200 daily.

Kettle Corn business

Income
$300
Expense
$100

Figure 11.6: Kettle Corn Business

Source: Author

With some success, Mike decides to take his business further. He divided his earnings into 100 shares. Each share costs $2. In other words, the *earning per share* is $2.

So, let's say, you walked past Mike's Kettle Corn business one day and decided to buy one share. Each share will give you a passive income of 20 cents per day. It is a good deal, right?

However, since there are only 100 shares offered to the public, the price of the share will be subject to the demand and supply. By the time you arrived at the shopping centre, the price of the share had become $20 per share, instead of $2 per share.

So, for now, how do you know if a share of Kettle Corn business is a good deal or not?

The first thing to do is to start by comparing it with other businesses.

The point is that price tells you very little thing about the intrinsic value of a stock. Stock with a higher price does not mean it is more valuable. Instead of looking at the price, you should be asking how much investors are willing to pay for each $1 in earning of a company in the market.

Kettle Corn business

Furniture business

Flower business

$2 earning per share

$10 earning per share

$1 earning per share

Share price
$20

Share price
$50

Share price
$5

Figure 11.7: P/E Ratio between three businesses

Source: Author

If you divide the price of stock by the *earning per share* for the companies above, you will find out that Kettle Corn Business has a P/E Ratio of 10, while the Furniture Business and Flower business has a P/E Ratio of 5. In other words, the market value is $5 for each $1 earning in the companies. If you decide to pay for Kettle Corn business, you are overpaying for its earnings.

Always remember the price in here is what investors are willing to pay for a stock. The earning is how much money a company makes. The P/E ratio tells you how much you are paying for the earning. It tells you whether a stock is overvalued or undervalued.

Robert J. Shiller of Yale University gathered data from the S&P500 from 1870 to today.

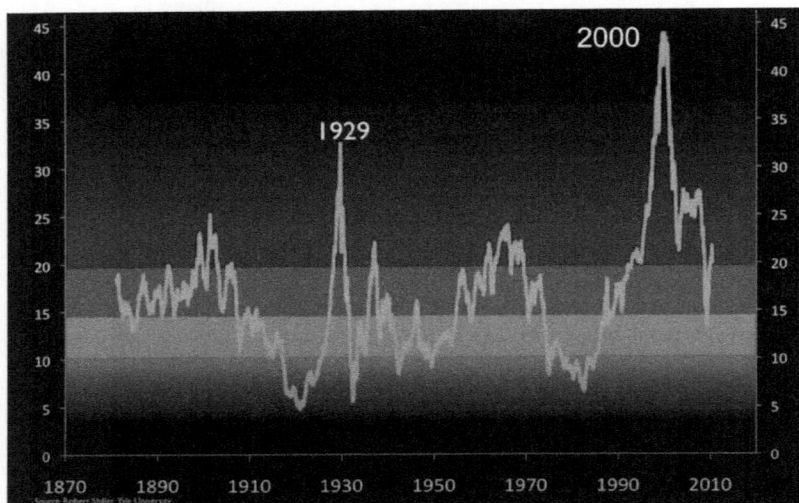

Figure 11.8: PE Ratio of S&P 500

Source: Robert J. Shiller of Yale University

What he found is that market valuation is defined into four categories:

PE Ratio	Valuation
<10	Undervalue
10-15	Fair Market Value
15-20	Overvalue
>20	Bubble

In 2000, just before the dotcom bubble burst, Nasdaq stocks traded at a staggering price-earnings ratio of 189.7. Investors that caught up with the mania were willing to buy stocks that had little to no earnings.

Eventually, the dotcom bubble burst.

So, how can we learn from the mistake in the dotcom bubble?

How can investors apply PE ratio when investing in stock?

Let me give you another example. Jane's Jewellery Pty Ltd has a $2 earning per share, with a share price of $20. John's Clothing Pty Ltd has a $1.5 earning per share, with a share price of $15. Their P/E ratios are the same, which is 10. Investors are willing to pay $10 for $1 of earning.

Now, suppose there is a third company called Foxy Supermarket that has $3 earning per share, with a share price of $60 and has a PE ratio 20. Before you invest in Foxy Supermarket, you have to ask yourself what is the potential of this company that investors are willing to pay $20 for a dollar in earning, as opposes to $10.

[Note: There are two additional types of P/E ratio: trailing P/E and forward P/E. Trailing P/E is the P/E ratio based on the last 12 months of actual earning. Forward P/E refers to the P/E ratio based on estimated future earnings.]

Besides the PE ratio, we also want to look at PEG. Say, for example, if Jane's Jewellery Pty Ltd has a PE ratio of 10 and a growth of 20%, then the PEG is 0.5. On the other hand, if John's Clothing Pty Ltd has a PE ratio of 10 and a growth of 10%, then the PEG is 1.

In reality, the lower the PEG, the better. It means you get more value of growth out of the money you invest in a company. The key point is, price is what you pay, and PEG is how much you are willing to pay for the earning and growth of the company. Always focus on PE ratio and PEG when picking a stock. Don't just look at the price. Study the financial statement of a company. This way, you will get a better return for your dollar invested.

[Note: the SEC requires each listed company to file a 10-Q statement each quarter, which has fundamental information about the company.]

Technical Analysis

While fundamental analysis is an X-ray for you to examine the financial health of a company, it is not enough information for you to invest. Not yet. The fundamentals of a company can lie. If you recall the Enron scandal in October 2001, the company had very good figures on paper. Enron was a very powerful company and had a strong financial statement. It had high growth, good revenue, low debt. It was a company laser focus on earning per share. Anyone from 1998 to October 2000 would think it would be foolish not to invest in Enron.

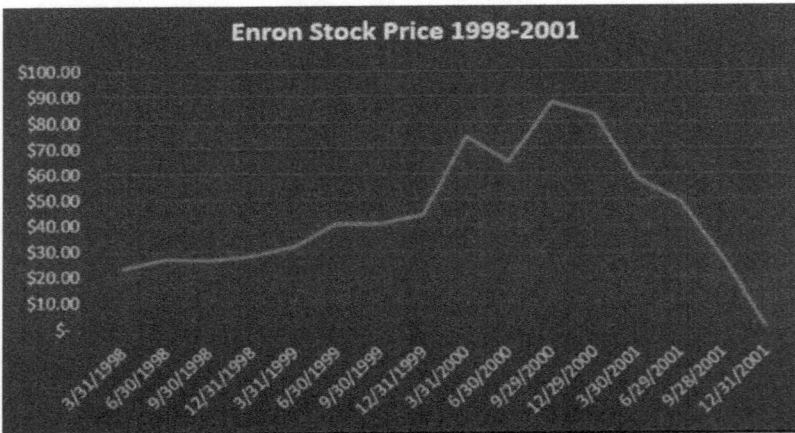

Figure 11.9: Enron Stock Price

Source: Enron

So, what happened in Enron accounting? How come people who only look at fundamental analysis couldn't find this out from the company's revenue?

The truth is, Enron used a technique called *mark to market accounting* that adjusts the value of an asset and liabilities. In a nutshell, it did a trick in accounting to recognize revenue when it had no revenue.

So, that is why you need to know another piece of important

information called technical analysis. Technical analysis is about the study of the market. Basically, it is an analysis about the supply and demand of a stock in the market. It is about what investors felt about the price of a stock in the past, and what is the *likelihood* of its price moving in a certain direction in the future?

In Technical analysis, we look at trends in charts.

Over a long period, typically, there are three types of trends:

1.   Up trend,

2.   Down trend,

3.   Sideways trend

An uptrend happens when there is a low supply and high demand of stocks.

Figure 11.10: Uptrend

Source: Author

A downtrend happens when there is a high supply and low demand of stocks.

Figure 11.11: Downtrend

Source: Author

A sideways trend happens when the stock price stays stagnant.

Figure 11.12: Sideway Trend

Source: Author

Trends are like waves. In investing, trends are your best friend. You can study trends in technical analysis to analysis any market, not just for stock. Regardless of real estate, stock, precious metals, commodity, it is important to look at the trends.

Support and Resistance

The first concept in technical analysis I want to talk about is the concept of *support* and *resistance*. The *support line* is the price where investors think a stock is of good value. It is like a floor on how low the price of a stock can get. The *resistance line* is the highest price investors can accept. It is like a ceiling of a stock price.

If you look at the chart from left to right, you will realize that there are old and new support and resistance levels. Behind the scenes, the market makers adjust the price up based on the demand and supply of a stock.

So, a rise in price means investors continue to accept the increase in price until it reaches a point where they think it is too expensive.

When investors change their attitude and say no to it, the *market makers* will adjust the price down based on the current demand and supply. When this happen, the stock price will fall until it reaches a point where there is enough support again.

As you may have noticed in the diagram below, there are new levels and old levels of support and resistance in an uptrend. This happens because investors have different opinions over time. When the number of buyers exceeds sellers, the price will rise.

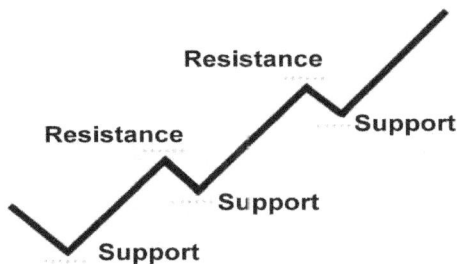

Figure 11.13: Support and Resistance in an uptrend

Source: Author

For example, ABC company has a support level of $50 and a resistance level of $70. With this information, Mary decides to purchase 1000 shares of ABC Company at a price of $51. She thinks it is a good buying opportunity. Based on technical analysis, ABC Company's share is unlikely to break its support line but has more upside potential. By understanding support and resistance, short-term traders are more likely to make profitable deals.

Swing High and Swing Low

Once you understand support and resistance, the next technical indicators you want to understand is swing high and swing low. In any uptrend, seldom will price go one-way. It will rise and hit resistance, pull back to support, and take another attempt to break the old resistance level until it reaches a new resistance level. It moves in a zig-zag fashion.

If you look at the figure below, you can visualize it as a series of mountain peaks and valleys. A *swing high* is a peak – the price reaches a peak before it declines. A *swing low* is a valley – the price reaches a bottom before it rises.

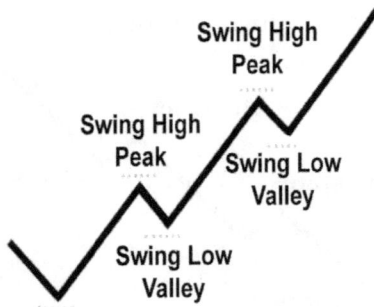

Figure 11.14: Swing High and Swing Low

Source: Author

A trend is considered an uptrend when we have a series of higher swing high and swing lows. Conversely, a downtrend means we have a series of lower and lower swing high and swing low. In fact, when a new swing high fails to form a higher swing because of market resistance, this is telling us the possibility of signs of a downtrend.

A sideways trend happens when swing high and swing low are bouncing back and forth in a channel. Neither of them manages to break the support and resistance levels.

Head and Shoulder

A head and shoulder pattern is one of the most reliable technical indicators in technical analysis. If you look at the figure below, does that look like a person with a left and right shoulder and a head in the middle?

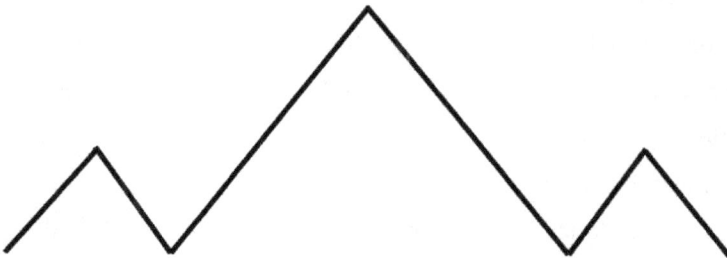

Figure 11.15: Head and Shoulder

Source: Author

A head and shoulder pattern is a trend reversal indicator. It indicates a downward trend is developing. There is a high probability that the price will break the support on the right hand side of the head and shoulder pattern.

Inverse Head and Shoulder

Inverse head and shoulder pattern is an indicator that works the exact opposite of the head and shoulder indictor. It indicates the development of an uptrend.

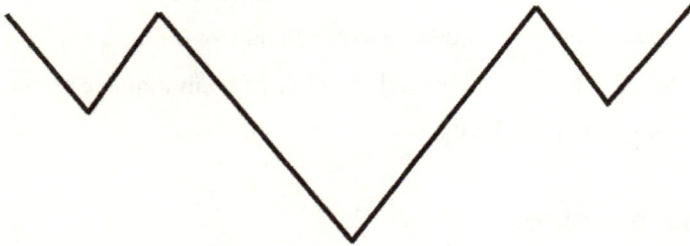

Figure 11.16: Inverse Head and Shoulder

Source: Author

Double Top

Double top means two-failed attempts to break a resistance level. However, a double top pattern tells us nothing about a trend. Not yet. It indicates a *likelihood* of a downward trend or an end of up trend. However, it is not recommended to use double top as an indicator as a false reading would lead to exit a position too early. Think of double top as an alarm only. The alarm might be real, and it might be false. Either way, a double top pattern should make you cautious. Wait for the confirmation that it will break the support before you sell.

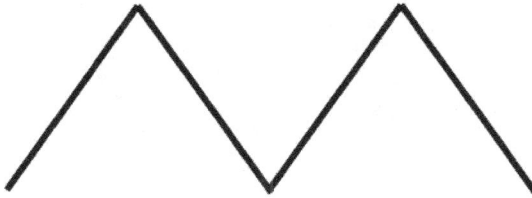

Figure 11.17: Double Top

Source: Author

Double Bottom

Double bottom is exactly the opposite of double top. It indicates a *likelihood* of an up trend or the end of a down trend. Again, when you see this happen, wait for the confirmation that it will break the resistance level before you buy.

Figure 11.18: Double Bottom

Source: Author

Ascending Triangle

An ascending triangle is a pattern that investors continue to say no to a resistance. However, each time the price falls and bounces back, they have a higher support level. An ascending triangle is a bullish formation that indicates a breakout might happen when the resistance line is broken.

Figure 11.19: Ascending Triangle

Source: Author

Descending Triangle

A descending triangle is a pattern that investors continue to say no to a support. However, each time the price falls and bounces back, they have a lower resistance level. A descending triangle is a bearish formation that indicates a breakout might happen when the support line is broken.

Figure 11.20: Descending Triangle

Source: Author

Cup and Handle

A cup and handle pattern is a very bullish indicator.

If you examine the silver chart in the figure below, do you see the cup shape, or U shape, from 1984 to 2007? Does this downward drift between 2008 and 2009 resemble a handle to you?

After a break out from 2009, silver rose from $8 to above $45 in just 2 years.

Figure 11.21: Cup and Handle Pattern

Source: Metastock

Moving Average

Moving average (MA) is a technical indicator that refers to the average trading price of an asset over a specified period. MA is used by investors or traders to identify trends through smoothing day-to-day price fluctuations to form trend lines. There are different moving average lengths. The most common ones are 15 days, 20 days, 30 days, 50 days, 100 days and 200 days. A 5-day moving average is calculated by adding the price data of an asset over the 5 days divided by 5.

Stock Investing Strategies

Once you have gathered enough information from fundamental and technical analysis, the next step is to position yourself.

Unlike real estate, the problem when you invest in the stock market is the lack of control. We cannot change how a company is being run and how the market reacts. However, what you can do is to position yourself and have the willingness to change your position when information changes. Once you understand this concept, you will realize there is no such thing as a good or bad market, all that matters is how you position yourself and manage the risk.

Long and Short

There are two positions in investing in stock: long position and short position.

If you buy a stock, you long stock. If you buy real estate with all cash, you long real estate. When you buy gold, you long gold. When you buy the U.S. dollar, you long the U.S. dollar. A long position means you buy an asset to hold it to hope it will rise. The worst long position is a position that continues to lose value every year. Unfortunately, this is exactly what most people do. They long local currency that is designed to lose value.

To short an asset, you are entering a *short position* by borrowing it from person A to sell it to person B. When the asset falls in value, you exit a short position by buying it back and return it to person A. For example, Jack knows that the price of XYZ is going to go down, so he decided to call his stockbroker to short one share of XYZ. His stock broker will then look for his database or contact other brokers to see if there is a client holding one share of XYZ. Then he borrows it from

Mary's portfolio and sells one share of XYZ in the market for Jack. Imagine XYZ was trading for $100. This will be credited to Jack's brokerage account. And if the stock price drops to $70, Jack calls his broker to cover his position of XYZ. The broker will then use the $100 in Jack's brokerage account to buy back XYZ stock valued at $70, and return this this stock to Mary's portfolio. Jack made $30 in profit by shorting selling.

To short an asset has higher risk compared to long an asset. When you buy a stock for $100, the most you lose is $100. Shorting is different because there is no way to tell how high a stock might rise. As the price goes up, your losses go up. This is no limit as to how much you can lose.

Call and Put Options

In the last chapter, we talked about options in real estate. It is the right but not the obligation to buy a property at a specified price within a specified time frame. That option is called a call option. When you use a *call option*, you are expecting the price to go up.

In stock, there is another option called a *put option*. It is the right but not the obligation to sell a specified amount of an underlying security at a specified price within a specified timeframe.

Call option and put options are derivatives. Their values are based on the underlying asset.

But what are derivatives?

Say, for example, orange skin is a derivative of an orange. Orange peels are derivative of an orange. Similarly, an option is a derivative of a stock. Its value derives from the stock.

But what is the purpose of using option in stock?

The answer is: Leverage.

Let's say you buy stock XYZ at a value of $100. Three months later, it increased to $110. When you sell, your ROI is 10%.

As a sophisticated investor, you want to improve this ROI. You want a higher return of investment. If you still remember the formula of ROI, it is the profit divided by the cost of investment. The smaller the amount you put into a deal, the higher the ROI.

$$ROI = \frac{Profit}{Cost\ of\ Investment}$$

I remember back in the mid 80s to early 90s, when my parents used to tell me how easily they made money in the stock market. It is like you can literally blindfold a man and ask him to randomly pick a few stocks in the Hang Seng Index, and they can easily make 100% or 200%. All you needed to do was to participate. However, this is not the case today.

Today, you need to know how to use leverage. I don't mean margin where you borrow to buy stock. What I mean is a very unique kind of leverage called options.

When you buy an option, you need to take three things into account:

1.   Strike price

2.   Expiration date

3.   Premium

In a call option, the *strike price* is the price of a stock that can be bought by the option holder. In a put option, the *strike price* is the price of a stock that can be sold by the option holder. The *expiry date* is the day when the option expires. As for *premium*, it refers to the price of the option contact the option seller is asking for.

Let me give you an example. CBA last traded at $68.66. If you believe the market will go up, you are going to look for a call option.

Code	Last	$+/-	% Chg	Bid	Offer	Open	High	Low	Volume	Options
CBA	68.660 ∧	1.000	1.48%	68.650	68.660	68.170	68.840	67.910	2,738,177	Options

Figure 11.22: Commonwealth Bank Stock CBA

Source: ASX

Below is a table called the option chain. It is an option matrix that listed all available option contracts for a security, such as stock. What you want to look at is an option with a strike price around $68.88, with say, 6 months left for expiry. In this case, pick call option CBAX68.

So, when you buy CBAX68, you are buying a call option with a strike price of $69 at premium of $4.435, expiring on 17th December 2020.

[Note: A relatively conservative investor might opt for a call option strike price at or below the stock price, while a trader with a high tolerance for risk may prefer a strike price above the stock price.]

Code	Expiry date	P/C	Exercise	Bid	Offer	Last
CBAWW8	17/12/2020	Call	67.000	5.425	5.425	0.000
CBAJ37	17/12/2020	Call	68.000	0.000	0.000	5.040
CBAXG9	17/12/2020	Call	68.010	4.805	4.805	0.000
CBAX68	17/12/2020	Call	69.000	4.435	4.435	0.000

Figure 11.23: Commonwealth Bank Option Chain

Source: ASX

[Note: The exercise price is the same as the strike price of an option. When you buy option contracts, you have to pay the ask price. When you write them, you receive the bid price. The option premium basically refers to either the price you pay to buy (*i.e. ask price*) or the price you receive for writing. (*i.e. bid price*)]

Since the standard number of shares covered by one option is 100, when you are buying CBAX68, you are essentially buying this option for $444 ($4.435 x 100) to have an option to buy 100 CBA shares at $69 per share before 17th December 2020.

Say, if CBA goes up to $77.43 by 17th December 2020, your option would have $8.43 ($77.43 - $69) of intrinsic value for each 100 shares. The $4.435 option you bought can be sold in the open market for $8.43. Your option effectively has an ROI of 100% with just a 12.8% rise in the underlying stock price.

And if CBA doubles to $137 per share before expiration, the $4.435 option you bought can be sold in the open market for $68. ($137 - $69). Your call option would have an insane ROI of 1433%, a 14 fold return!

Below is an option profit and loss diagram. It is a great way to visualize your option strategy. The maximum loss of this call option, CBAX68, is limited to the premium paid and the commission. Therefore, no matter low the price drops, your maximum loss is going to be $444 (point C). The breakeven point stock price for a call option is that call option strike price plus the premium paid, which is $73.44 ($69 +$4.435). When the stock price increases to $73.43 (a 6.4% increase), you break even. Beyond that point, you can see the power of using leverage with option. For just a 13.6% increase in stock price, you are effectively doubling your money.

Breakeven Stock Price = Call Option Strike Price + Premium

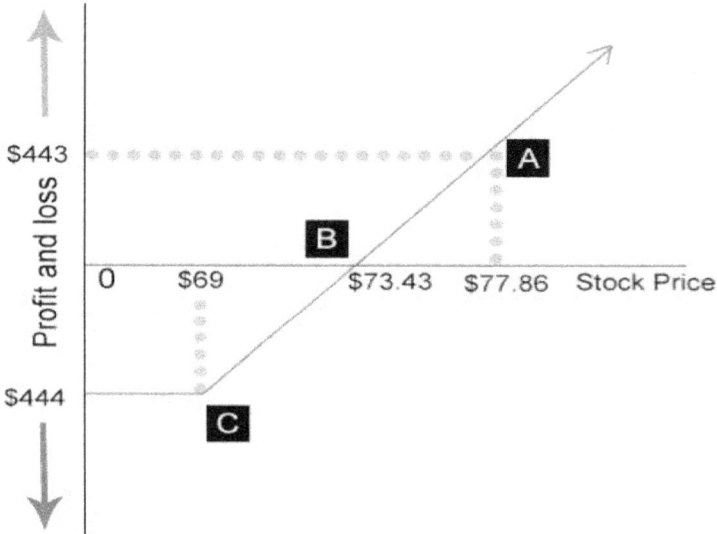

Figure 11.24: Call Option Profit and Loss Diagram

Source: Author

New Stock Price	Strike Price	% rise in stock	Premium	New Option Price	Profit from selling option (Each option has 100 shares)	Option ROI
$73.43	$69	6.4%	$4.43	$4.43	0	0
$74.43	$69	7.8%	$4.43	$5.43	$100	23%
$75.43	$69	9.31%	$4.43	$6.43	$200	45%
$76.43	$69	10.7%	$4.43	$7.43	$300	67%
$77.43	$69	12.2%	$4.43	$8.43	$400	90%
$78.43	$69	13.6%	$4.43	$9.43	$500	112%

Table 11.1: Option ROI

Source: Author

[Note: For a simplified explanation, I have excluded the commission in this example.]

Option is not risk free. When you buy an option at point C, the share price of the stock needs to move to point B before you can break even. In the case of CBA, it needs to move 6.4% before the expiry date.

Before you get excited, it is important to understand some more important concepts about the value of an option. Earlier, we talked about premiums, which is the price of an option. We also understand that price is different from value. Say, if the *strike price* of CBA is $69, and the share price moves to $72, the *intrinsic value* of the option will be $3. So, when you buy a call option, you may realize that some of them already have an intrinsic value because their strike price is lower than the stock price.

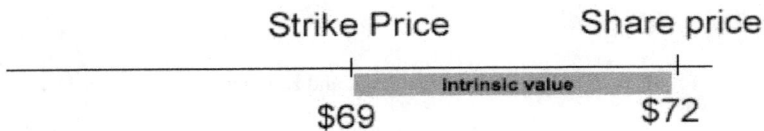

Intrinsic value = Share price – strike price

Say, for example, if a call option is selling a premium at $4.43, and the *intrinsic value* of the option is only $3, then why are you overpaying a premium?

That is where extrinsic value comes into play. The difference between the premium and the intrinsic value of an option is called extrinsic value. In this case, the extrinsic value is $1.43 ($4.43 - $3).

Extrinsic Value = Premium – Intrinsic Value
Premium = Time Value + Implied Volatility

An extrinsic value of an option is the *time value* of an option adds *implied volatility value*. Unlike stock, where you can hold it for a long time, an option has an expiry date. It has a time value attached to it. The value of CBAX68 depends on how much time is left before the expiry date. The longer the expiry date, the more the time value of an option costs. Implied volatility means the expected volatility of a stock over the life of an option. The more volatile the stock price moves, the higher the premium is going to be. So when implied volatility increases after a trade has been placed, it's good for the option owner and bad for the option seller. Be careful that a change in implied volatility can create loss in a call option even if you are right about the stock's direction.

Below is a short summary of what we have discussed so far. There are two methods to invest in stock when the stock price goes up.

First option: Buy share
- You bought 100 shares CBA at $69 per share for $6,900.
- By 17th December 2020, the stock price doubled to $138.
- You sell the 100 CBA shares for $13,800 and make a profit of $6,900. This is a 100% ROI.

Second option: Buy Call option
- You buy a call option of CBA with a strike price of $69, with a premium of $4.43, and an expiry date - 17th December 2020. The total cost is $443.
- By 17th December 2020, the stock price doubled to $138.
- The option has an intrinsic value of $69.
- You sell the CBA call option for a profit of $6,457. [($69-$4.43) x 100 shares]
- This is a ROI of 1357%.

So, far, we have talked about how to use call option to make money when the market is going up. How about when the market goes down?

Put option gives you the ability to protect yourself or leverage to take advantage of a down market. Let me give you another example. Suppose we did a technical analysis on CBA and decided that the stock will trend down.

Code	Last	$+/-	% Chg	Bid	Offer	Open	High	Low	Volume	Options
CBA	68.660 ∧	1.000	1.48%	68.650	68.660	68.170	68.840	67.910	2,738,177	Options

Figure 11.25: Commonwealth Bank Stock CBA

Source: ASX

The next step is to look at the option chain and find an option with the strike price close to the stock price. We pick CBAX78 in this case.

Since each option has 100 shares, we buy this option for $559 ($5.585 x 100) to have an option to sell 100 CBA shares at $69 per share before 17th December 2020. This is the maximum amount you can lose if the stock price rises, which is point C.

Code	Expiry date	P/C	Exercise	Bid	Offer	Last
CBAJ47	17/12/2020	Put	68.000	5.115	5.115	0.000
CBAXT9	17/12/2020	Put	68.010	5.105	5.105	0.000
CBAX78	17/12/2020	Put	69.000	5.585	5.585	0.000
CBAXV9	17/12/2020	Put	69.010	5.590	5.590	0.000

Figure 11.26: Commonwealth Bank Put Option Chain

Source: ASX

Point B is the breakeven point. When the CBA falls by 8.1% by the expiry date, the put option break-even. The break-even price is calculated by the put option strike price minus the premium.

Breakeven Stock Price = Put Option Strike Price - Premium

If the stock price continues to fall to $60.415 by 17th December 2020, your option would have $8.585 ($69 - $60.415) intrinsic value for each 100 shares. And the $5.585 option you bought can be sold in the open market for $8.585. Your option's ROI is effectively 54% with just a 12.4% drop in the underlying stock price. And if the share price of CBA falls by 18.24%, the ROI of your put option will have 125%. You effectively more than doubled your money.

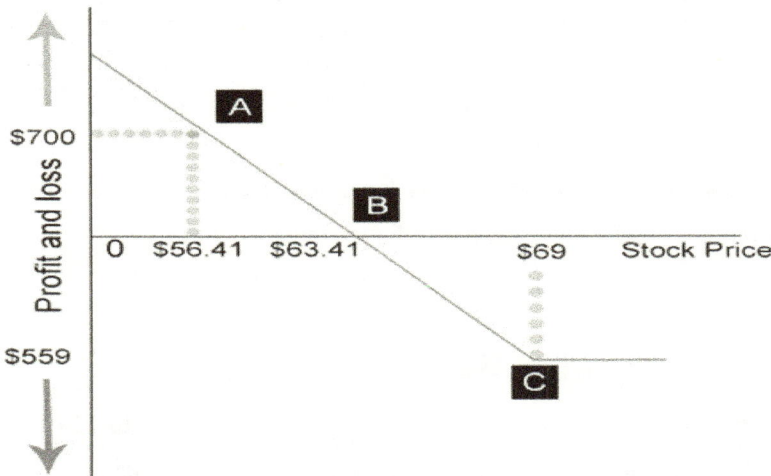

Figure 11.27: Put Option Profit and Loss Diagram

Source: Author

New Stock Price	Strike Price	% Falls in stock	Premium	New Option Price	Profit from selling option (Each option has 100 shares)	Option ROI
$63.415	$69	8.1%	$5.585	$5.585	0	0
$62.415	$69	9.5%	$5.585	$6.585	$100	18%
$61.415	$69	11%	$5.585	$7.585	$200	36%
$60.415	$69	12.4%	$5.585	$8.585	$300	54%
$59.415	$69	13.9%	$5.585	$9.585	$400	72%
$58.415	$69	15.3%	$5.585	$10.585	$500	90%
$57.415	$69	16.79%	$5.585	$11.585	$600	107%
$56.415	$69	18.24%	$5.585	$12.585	$700	125%

Table 11.2: Option ROI

Source: Author

Below is a short summary of what we have discussed so far. There are two methods to invest in stock when the stock price goes down.

First option: Short share
- You short 100 shares CBA at $69 per share for $6,900.
- By 17th December 2020, the stock price drop by half to $34.5.
- You buy back the 100 CBA shares for $3,450, and make a profit of $3,450. This is a 100% ROI.

Second option: Sell Put Option
- You buy a put option of CBA with a strike price of $69, with a premium of $5.585, and an expiry date - 17th December 2020. The total cost is $559.
- By 17th December 2020, the stock price drop by half to $34.5.
- The put option has an intrinsic value of $34.5.

- You sell the CBA put option for a profit of $2,891. [($34.5-$5.585) x 100 shares]
- This is a ROI of 417%.

A put option is like an insurance policy. If you bought 100 shares of CBA at $69 each for $6,900, and you have bought a put option as described above, you are covered. For example, if CBA plunged to $9 by 17th December, that guy who sold you the put option will have to buy back 100 shares from you at $69, even when CBA is now $9 per share.

Both the put and call options allow you to put down a smaller initial cost of investment, lower your down payment significantly, and achieve a higher ROI. This is the power of leverage.

Long, short, put and call options are how you position yourself based on the fundamental and technical analysis. And by using options to leverage, you are magnifying your gain and lowering your risks only to the cost of the options.

Writing an option

Apart from buying and selling options, the owner of shares can also choose to write their own options. If Mary had 100 shares of CBA at $69 per share, and she thinks the market is going to increase in the long run, she can write call options for the shares she holds. In this case, her option is called a *covered call option*.

Say, for example, Mary wrote a call option with a strike price of $69 and a premium of $3, and if the stock goes up to $79, Mary earns a nice profit because she bought low and sold high. On the other hand, if the stock goes sideways or down, Mary can earn cash flow from the call option's premium (i.e. $3 x 100) because there is always going to be someone who bought the call option, thinking the market was going to go up, but guessed it incorrectly.

While writing *covered call options* means you to have actual share for delivery, writing *naked call option* means you are selling options without underlying shares. A naked call option is not recommended, as it can be very dangerous. If you sell the call option without owning the underlying stock, and the call is exercised by the buyer, you will be left with a short position in the stock. There is no limit on how much you can potentially lose! So, only write covered options.

Hedging

How to mitigate your risk is a skill in investing that's too important to ignore. Investing without risk management is like driving a car without a seatbelt on. It is like buying a house and not buying fire insurance.

If you want to be successful in investing in stock, first, you must increase your chance of winning by performing fundamental analysis and technical analysis. Second, you must learn how to leverage, position yourself, as well as to manage risk to reduce your chance of losing.

To manage risk, we need to be able to identify it first.

In the stock market, there are mainly two types of risks: non-systemic risks and systemic risks.

Non-systemic risk is a type of risk that affects an individual risk only. For example, if Honda suddenly announced the recall of vehicles manufactured between last year and this year, this is non-systemic, as it will affect Honda's stock price only.

A stockbroker will usually advise you to guard against risk by diversifying into other stock in other sectors. On the surface, this argument appears to make sense. But what the stockbroker didn't tell you is diversification in the same asset class, which is stock, is not useful against systemic risk.

So, what is a systemic risk?

A systemic risk is when the entire market drops, like the coronavirus epidemic in 2020. All stock plunges.

That is why you need to hedge against both non-systemic and systemic risks with insurance. One way to do so is by using put options. Another way to manage your risk is by having an exit strategy in place. This is done by *orders*.

So, what is an order?

An order is an instruction to buy or sell in a stock market. In order to control the risk, you want your orders to be executed when the stock price moves in a certain direction. In any trading venue, there are four different orders on how you control your positions.

1. Market order
2. Limit order
3. Stop-loss order or stop order
4. Stop limit order

A *market order* is an order to buy a security immediately. This type of order does not guarantee your order will be executed at the price you want to buy. If other orders are executed before your market order is executed, you will end up buying it at a higher price. So, it is best to avoid market order if you have a specific price point you want to get in.

A *limit order* is an order to buy or sell stock at a specific price more favourable than the limit price. It means you want to buy or sell a stock, but you have a limit as to how much you want to buy or sell for in your mind. For example, if you want to buy AAPL for no more than $280, you use a buy limit order. This will be executed when AAPL falls to $280 or below. Conversely, if you want to sell AAPL for no less than

$330, the sell limit order will be executed when AAPL hits $330 or higher. A limit order is not guaranteed to be executed if the stock reaches the limit price. This happens if the price moves too quickly.

A *stop-loss order* or *stop order* is an order placed with a broker to buy or sell once the stock reaches a certain price. There are two ways to use a stop order: one for entry and one for exit to limit an investor's loss on a position. For the first case, let's say, AAPL has been forming an ascending triangle pattern and is about to break out, and you want to buy at $280. To do so, place a buy stop order at $280. Once AAPL hits the stop buy price of $280, the order becomes a market order, and the trading system purchases the stock at the next available price point. A sell stop order, on the other hand, is to protect your loss. Say, for example, you bought AAPL for $310, and you placed a stop order loss at $300. Overnight, the price falls to $250. Your stop order loss will be triggered at $300 and become a market order, and will be sold at the next available price point is. Make sure you use it.

A *stop limit order* gives you very specific control on how you position. It combines the features of both a stop order and limit order. For a *stop limit order*, you need to enter both the stop price and the limit price. If the stock price hits the stop price, the *limit order* will be executed. Let's say XPA is trading between $45 and $65. You place a *buy stop limit order* to buy XPA with a stop price of $55 and a limit price of $50. When the XPA hits the stop price of $55, it will trigger a limit order to buy once the stock price drops again to $50. This allows you to buy the stock cheaper. For selling with a stop limit order, once the price drops down to the stop price you set, it will trigger a sell at whatever limit price you entered. Say, ABC is trading between $30 and $20 and is trending down. You decide to place a sell stop limit order by setting $25 at stop price and $23 at limit price. So, when ABC hits the stop price of $25, it will then trigger to sell the stock at no less than $24. However, if the price changes very rapidly, the stop limit order might not be fulfilled.

Besides orders, another important technique you want to know about is the reward to risk ratio. Whenever you decide to buy a stock, you study the stock with fundamental analysis and technical analysis. Next, you identify the entry price, exit price, the target-selling price and your reward/risk ratio. Say, for example, AAPL is currently trading at $310. You think the target price will be $330, and you then put a *stop-loss order* or *stop order* at $300. In this case, you are positioned to have a reward/risk ratio of 2:1.

$$(\$330-\$310): (\$310-\$300) = 2:1$$

In any trading, you want your stock performance to be at least 2:1 or higher. Over a number of trades, you will lose, and you will win. But you will come out better because you will profit twice as much as you lose if you position yourself this way.

To sum up, using reward to risk ratios, orders, options are ways you can hedge against the potential loss in a stock market. These tactics can dramatically allow you to take more control on your investment and not leave it to the mercy of the market.

Hidden Secrets of Options

Before wrapping up this chapter, I want to talk a bit more about options.

The legendary investor Warren Buffett discussed the topic of stock options in great detail in his 1985 letter to shareholders. He considered stock options the right reward to talented ones. With a net worth of $65 billion, Warren Buffett is probably the most successful investor of all time. Warren Buffett's Berkshire Hathaway Inc ended 2007 with $40 billions of exposure to 94 derivative contracts, collecting $7.6 premiums.

So, what techniques does he use in options that generate such huge profits?

One of the derivative tools he uses is put options. Here is how Buffett uses it. Suppose Buffett wants to buy AAPL, which is currently trading at $350 per share. Buffett did his fundamental and technical analysis, and decided to buy it at $300. Let's say, he sells one million put options with a $300 strike price for a premium of $2. This will mean an income of $2 million. Investors who are buying these put options are the ones who fear AAPL will go down.

Now, there are a few possible scenarios:

Scenario 1: If AAPL did fall below $300, Buffett would have to fulfil his promises and buy back the one million shares at $300 per share, which is what he desired in the first place. He will be a happy man.

Scenario 2: AAPL stays flat or rose above $350. Buffett would still be happy because he collected $2 million premium from selling one million put options valued at $2 per option premium.

Either scenario, Buffett had positioned himself well. He doesn't care whether the market goes up or down. He is happy no matter which way AAPL goes. By selling put options at a strike price lower than today's price, Buffett gets paid premiums upfront just by making a promise he will buy back a stock he wants at a lower price. The opposite is also true for writing call options for a stock that you want to sell at a higher price than it is today.

***

I hope this chapter has given you comprehensive steps on how to invest in the stock market with an edge. There are plenty of virtual trading accounts in stock market investing. I strongly encourage you to practice with them before actually jumping in to invest in the stock market. The more you practice, the more it becomes second nature to you.

Chapter 12

Hidden Secrets of Gold and Silver

So far, we have talked about two-asset classes - real estate and stocks. The third type of asset class that should be in every investor's portfolio is gold and silver. In my first two books, *Corruption of Real Money* and *Legacy of Debt*, I detailed the role of gold in monetary history and how the global dollar standard has become the new monetary system that replaces money with debt.

If you have lived through the financial crisis of 2008, and the most recent coronavirus epidemic in 2020, you will probably feel something isn't quite right with our economy.

If I were to give you an analogy about the current global economy outlook, I would describe it as a deflating balloon with many holes in it. Central banks and governments around the world have been printing currency like crazy to pump air back in to keep this balloon afloat.

Clearly, the global dollar standard is unsustainable. Our current monetary system is reaching the end of its lifespan. It is just a matter of time before our current monetary system will collapse. When that happens, the world will seek a new type of money to replace the dollar in the new monetary system. There will be an unprecedented wealth transfer in the history of mankind.

I believe gold will be the one and future money in this wealth transfer.

It will play a significant role in the new monetary system in the 21st century.

Gold and the U.S. Dollar

Gold is a direct competitor to the dollar. If you are investing in gold, then you are betting against the dollar. Below is a chart showing the correlation between the dollar index DXY and gold. Did you see the pattern of a cycle?

In the 90s, when the U.S. dollar flourished, gold was the most untouched and unloved asset. It was not until the U.S. dollar index peaked at $129 and began to decline in 2002 that gold began its bull market. From 2002 to 2012, gold had a decade of a bull run, and at the same time, the value of the dollar declined. Between the years 2012 to 2016, the gold market fell, while the dollar rose again. In 2019, the US index and gold had a rare simultaneous rise.

Figure 12.1: Gold Prices and U.S. Dollar index Correlation
Source: marcotrends.net

The Magic of DOW/ Gold Ratio

Once you understand the dynamics of the gold market and the dollar index, the next chart I want to show you is the Dow Jones Industrial Average (DOW) to the price of gold.

When you look at the points in DOW, we are looking at the price in USD. Price, however, is not a very good measurement. The Federal Reserve and central banks around the world can print dollars without limit. That is why you see the DOW keeps climbing while companies are making record low earnings. It is an illusion or worse, delusion. The more currency is printed, the faster the currencies we hold in our bank lose purchasing power.

So, instead of measuring the price of an asset, you as an investor should measure its value.

Since gold represents value, when you measure an asset against the price of gold, you are essentially eliminating the dollar and measuring the value of an asset in an ounce of gold. This is an important concept. You do not want to invest in an asset that is rising in price but falling in value.

Let me explain with an example. Imagine your great grandfather, John, bought 10 shares of DOW in the 1920s. Each share was worth $1,400. By 1929, right before the market crash, each share of DOW hit an all-time high of $5,152. But, instead of selling it, John held it all the way down to $807 during the Great Depression of the 1930. After this painful lesson, John decided he wants to hold it until the price one day goes back to the 1929 peak. And by 1959, after 19 long years, that one day finally happened. The DOW finally climbed back to its 1929 peak! But, again, John decided to continue holding onto his 10 shares of DOW because the stock broker told him the stock market will be going much higher.

By 1966, the market hit a peak of $7,550 and then plunged. John, once again, continued to hold all the way down. By 1982, he retired and sold his 10 shares of DOW at $2,365. John was still a very happy man. He told everyone about how he'd made 69% return on his investment. Do you want to be John? The truth is that John doesn't know if an investment is overvalued or undervalued. That is why he decided to buy and hold.

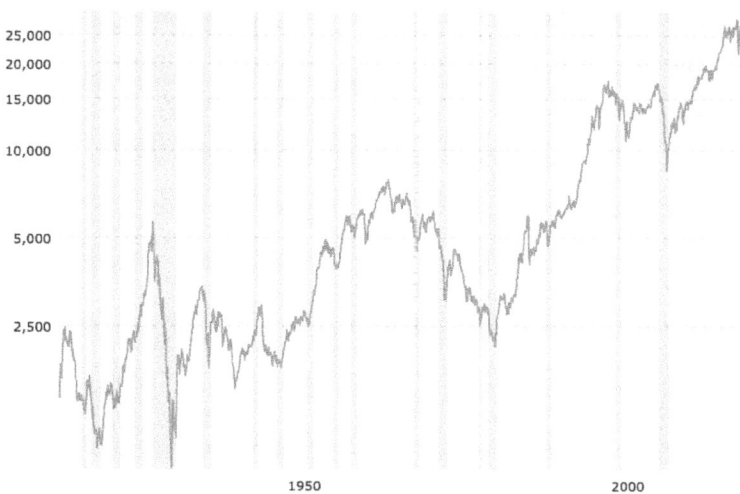

Figure 12.2: DOW

Source: marcotrends.net

Now, let's have a look at your other great grandfather John in a parallel universe. John understood that price is nothing, but value is everything. Instead of looking at the DOW in the media, he made his own chart to price the DOW in gold. He called it the DOW to Gold ratio – an indicator to tell you how many ounces of gold it would take to buy a share of DOW. Let's say, John, bought 10 shares of DOW in the 1920s. Each share is worth $1,400. He studied the DOW/Gold ratio the whole time. By 1929, John realized that the DOW was too overvalued because it took 16 ounces of gold to buy 1 share of DOW. So, he sold all his 10 shares

for 160 ounces of Gold instead. By 1930, the Great depression happened.
The Dow/Gold ratio plunged to an all-time low of 2. Realizing this was
an opportunity while everyone was trying to wait for the market to go
back up, John sold his 160 ounces of gold and bought 80 shares of the
DOW. John positioned himself to be a very happy man. Knowing the
DOW/Gold ratio peaked at 16, he decided to sell his 80 shares at around
that peak in 1958 for $400,000, with each share of DOW worth $5,000
per share. That is a ROI of 28,471%!

So, you see, by understanding the magic of the DOW/Gold ratio, this
John made a fortune, while the other John barely broke even.

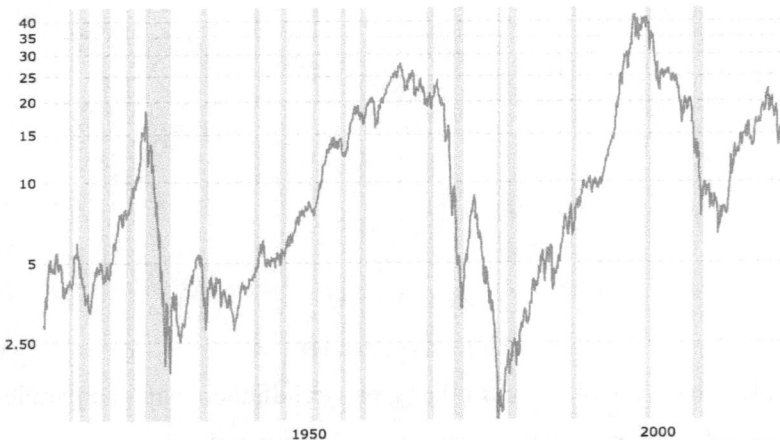

Figure 12.3: DOW gold ratio

Source: marcotrends.net

In fact, besides real estate, it is worth mentioning that if you invest in
one and only one asset class, you are unlikely be able to take advantage
of the magic above. You can invest in one thing for a very, very long
time and end up nowhere. But, if you can measure whether something
is overvalue or undervalue and have a willingness to sell the overvalue

asset class and buy the undervalue asset class; you are on the road to true wealth. This is the main reason why this book talks about all investment asset classes.

Real Estate to Gold ratio

Conventional wisdom taught us that home prices will always go up. It gets more expensive because of demand and supply.

But, when you look at it in terms of value, not the price, you will see a very different picture.

In 1973, the price of a U.S. median home cost about $40,000. The price of gold at the beginning of 1973 was $65 per ounce. If you price a home in gold, it would have cost you 615 ounces of gold to buy a home back in 1973.

Fast forward to 1980, and the average price of a U.S. median home climbed to $63,700. However, the price of gold hit $850. So, the value of a home in gold crashed to just 74.9 ounces!

Did you see the opportunity?

If you look at the price of the U.S. house in history, the price of real estate in 1973 seems to be a bargain. However, if you measure the price of house in gold, that undervalued home is overvalued. If you already owned a property before 1973, and you sell it and convert it into gold, you would own 615 ounces of gold. And by 1980, you sell your gold and convert it to real estate, you could have bought 8 properties outright, no down payment!

Today, once again, real estate is overvalued if you measure it in gold. That is one reason why you should accumulate precious metals. When the real estate to gold ratio reverses this time, it is going to be the biggest wealth transfer in history. If you own gold, you can buy real estate very inexpensively. It is just history repeating.

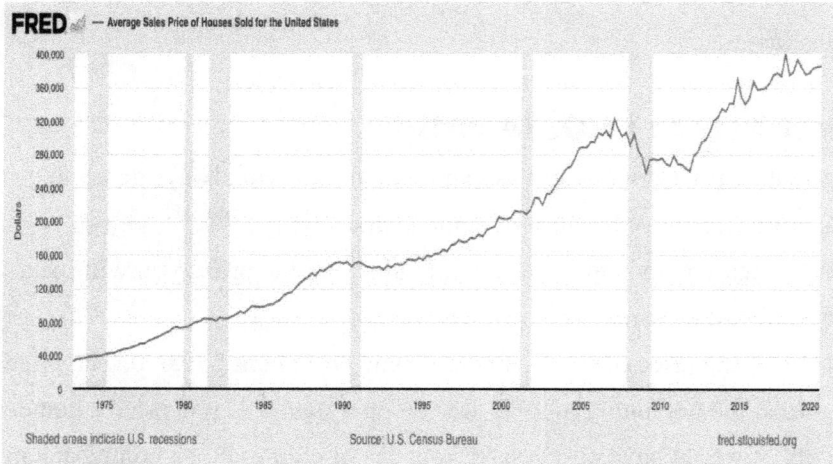

Figure 12.4: Average Sales Price of Houses in the U.S

Source: U.S. Census Bureau

Figure 12.5: Gold Price

Source: U.S. Census Bureau

Gold to Silver Ratio

Besides gold, a better opportunity is its cousin – silver. Historically, gold and silver have been used as money consistently for more than 6,000 years. They became de facto money around 600 BC when they were struck in Lydian coins as stores of value used for trade.

Throughout history, gold and silver has a very stable ratio of 16:1. It means silver is 16 times more abundant than gold. As you can see from the chart below, the gold to silver price ratio (G/S Ratio) has a natural average of 16 from 1687 to pre-1900. In 1972, the U.S. government fixed this ratio at 15:1 with the Mint Act of 1792. However, as we entered the 20th century, you can see that the G/S ratio began to fluctuate. With the discovery of massive amounts of silver in the U.S., the government attempted to manipulate the price of gold, and the average G/S ratio in the 20th century became 47: 1.

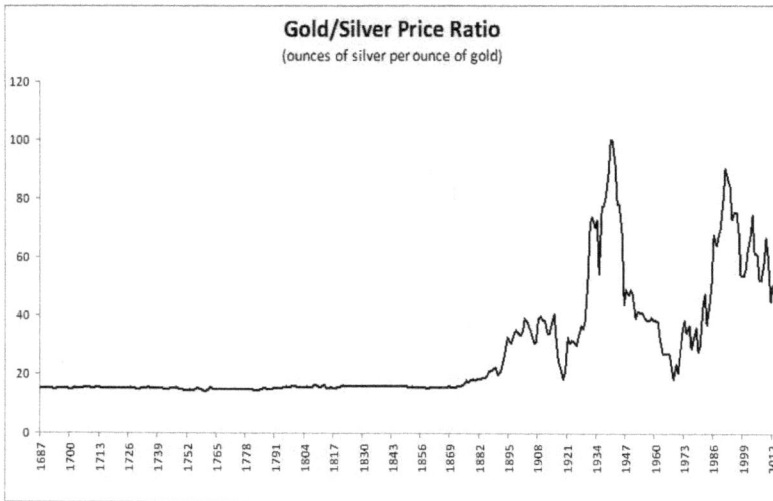

Figure 12.6: Gold to Silver Price Ratio

Source: seekingalpha.com

Unlike gold, which can be expensive for an average investor to get in, silver is more affordable. An ounce of gold today costs about $1,684 USD, but for silver, it costs only $17.61 USD. That's why silver is recognized as the poor man's gold.

Gold and silver have very high correlation most of the time, but not all the time. In certain times, silver price lags gold price. Silver's underperformance can be seen by using the G/S ratio.

The truth is that real precious metal investors do not buy gold and silver based on the price. They buy it based on the G/S ratio. When the G/S ratio is high, it is an indicator for a precious metal investor to sell gold to buy silver. On the contrary, if the G/S ratio is low, it is an opportunity to sell back the silver and convert it to gold.

An Accident Waiting to Happen

Among all asset classes, silver is the most undervalued asset class in the 21st century.

No asset class today is trading below their historic high, except silver.

Figure 12.7: Silver price

Source: silverprice.org

But, unlike other asset classes, the silver market tends to be very volatile. The dynamic of the silver market can catch investors by surprise. The price of silver can stay sideways for a very long time and speed up very, very quickly when it reaches the end of the precious metal cycle.

As I am writing now in 2020, the G/S ratio is trading between 90 and 120. This range of high G/S ratio is unprecedented any time in history. It is telling investors that silver is incredibly undervalued compared to gold. Like any other cycle, the cycle of G/S ratio cycle will eventually reverse to the mean. When that happens, it will overshoot to the downside to a potentially historically low G/S ratio.

This shift in cycle signals the end of the current precious metal market cycle.

Ultimately, the purchasing power of gold and silver will rise exponentially when they catch up with the currencies that have been created.

It is an accident waiting to happen.

How to Invest in Precious Metal?

There are several ways you can include gold and silver in your investment portfolio. The most direct way is to purchase gold and silver in the form of bullion. Buying physical bullion is the recommended way to invest because there is a saying in the industry that if you don't hold in, you don't own it.

Bullion dealers are the distributors of gold and silver bullion. They bought their inventory from the government mint like the Perth Mint in Australia, the Royal Canadian Mint or the U.S. Mint. To place an order, you just need to either walk in to their store and buy it over the counter, or place the order online to have them delivered to you via the post.

Before you invest, you need to check the spot price of gold and silver. If you are buying physical metals, the dealer is going to charge you a premium on top of the spot price. This premium is the profit the dealer is going to make per transaction. The premiums charged will depend on what form of bullion you are buying.

There are two forms of bullion you can buy: coins and bars. For gold and silver bullion coins, the premium will be much higher because it is more liquid. The investment grade of both gold and silver bullion should be .999 or above, which should be engraved on the bullion. Personally, I would prefer to invest in government or LBMA accredited bullion coins and bars. The government has invested a lot of money to prevent counterfeiting of bullions. Also, when it comes to selling back to the dealer or the private market, government backed bullions are more liquid. It is much easier to sell back silver bullion like the American Silver Eagle than a third party silver round.

But buying physical metals has disadvantages as well. Firstly, you need to rent a bullion vault for private storage. Secondly, the premium charged on some bullion coins can be a lot. Silver Bullion coins like the Perth Mint Lunar series have numismatic value besides the value of silver. But this is a subject outside the scope of this book.

So, if you are a beginner, and you want to invest in silver I would recommend you to stick with the following:

1.   American Silver Eagle
2.   Canadian Silver Maple
3.   PAMP Silver 1kg bar

For gold, you can stick with gold coins like the American Gold Eagle or Canadian Gold Maple.

Always have a good understanding about the type of bullion you are going to buy. Research on the weight, thickness and pattern of the bullion you are going to buy. Lastly, always buy from accredited local dealers with a good reputation.

If you do not want to hold physical metal, but you want to gain exposure to gold and silver, you may also consider gold and silver ETFs (exchanged traded fund). Investing in ETF is the second best option, as it is more liquid compared to investing in physical metal. On top of that, you do not need to worry about the risk of an ongoing storage fee, but you'll need to pay an annual management fee, a brokerage fee and the bid/ask spread when buying or selling.

The third best option to expose your investment portfolio to gold and silver is investing in mining stock. It is not the same as investing in physical silver. The price of mining stock depends on the fundamental of the company, which may or may not have a strong correlation to the price of gold and silver.

***

I hope by now that you have a good general understanding of how to find out if an asset class is overvalued or undervalued by pricing it in ounces of gold. More importantly, I hope you find out about the potential of gold and silver. In my next book, *Wealth Cycles in Gold and Silver*, I will talk about how to invest in gold and silver in depth.

In my opinion, all investors should allocate 10% to 20% of their portfolio in investing in precious metal. If you are young and can take on more risk, buy more silver. If you are over 50 and have less risk tolerance, buy gold instead.

You might be wondering why you shouldn't invest everything you have in gold and silver if it sounds so compelling.

The reason is simple.

You do not know *when* the revaluation of gold and silver will happen. No one has a crystal ball. Indicators suggest the Global Dollar Standard is on its last legs. It is near. But again, near is subjective. It could be decades away. It is an accident waiting to happen. When the coronavirus epidemic happened in the first half of 2020, the probability of that accident happening is increasing every day.

That is why you should allocate a small portion of your income and invest in gold and silver every single month to hedge against inflation. Don't save everything in dollars.

Chapter 13

Hidden Secrets of Cryptocurrency

On 15th September 2008, Wall Street investment bank giant Lehman Brothers filed for insolvency. The stock market dropped worldwide. The U.S. economy slowed to a standstill. It was the global financial crisis of 2008. Coincidentally, just one month later, on 31st October 2018, an anonymous identity under the name of Satoshi Nakamoto published the Bitcoin whitepaper. In the whitepaper, Satoshi put forward a new approach to replace the traditional banking model – one that reduces the dependency on centralized banking, which fuelled the financial crisis.

Satoshi Nakamoto coins it the Bitcoin.

What is Bitcoin?

Bitcoin is the world's first peer-to-peer decentralized virtual currency that allows transactions over the Internet without going through a financial institution. It solves two major problems: trusts and double spending.

Bitcoin is separated into two components – a decentralized P2P network and the digital currency called BTC.

Unlike other government-issued currency, bitcoin is limited in supply.

It has a set maximum supply of 21 million coins and is not controlled by any entity.

Satoshi Nakamoto's idea behind Bitcoin is a consensus algorithm called Proof-of-Work or PoW using blockchain technology.

So, what is a blockchain?

A blockchain is literally a chain of block.

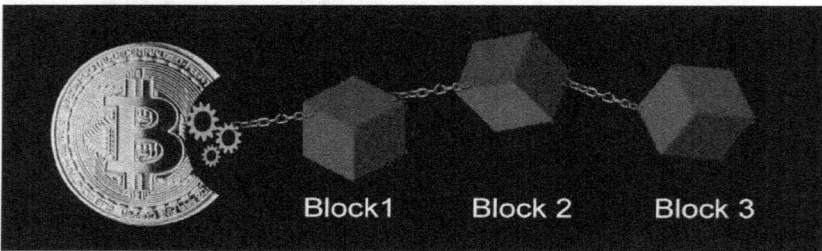

Figure 13.1: Blockchain Technology

Source: Author

Inside each block is a ledger that stores information about transactions like the date, time, amount, the digital signature of the buyer and seller, and a hash – a unique cryptographic code that distinguishes one block from another.

Each Bitcoin user has a Bitcoin wallet. Inside the Bitcoin wallet is a private key and a public address for receiving Bitcoin. The Bitcoin private key takes a central role in ownership and control of the cryptocurrencies inside. It exists as a series of randomly generated numbers and characters. Here is an example of what a bitcoin private key looks like.

2E99423A4ED27608AB5A2616A2B0E9E52CED330AC530EDC
C32C8FFC6A526AEDD

A public key, on the other hand, is a key generated from the private key. It is a cryptographic code made up of 26 to 34 characters. A public key is just like a bank account that allows the user to receive bitcoin in his or her account. It is shared in a blockchain, so the public can see it. When you lose your public key, don't worry. You can always use your private key to recreate it.

How Blockchain works?

When a new block is added to the blockchain, that transaction inside the block must be verified first. This is done with a PoW system using a network of computers.

Here is how it works: Inside the PoW system, computers in a P2P network will check that the transaction happened in a way you said it did. These computers are called miners. They will compete to confirm the detail of the purchase like the transaction time, date, the amount, the digital signatures of the buyer and seller and the hash, etc. by solving complex computational math problems.

Well, you may wonder why do computers have to solve maths problems for proof of work?

The reason is simple. By solving complex computational math problems, these miners have proven that they have done the check. That is why it is called PoW.

If a computer in the P2P network successfully solves this maths problem first, it will become eligible to add that block to the blockchain. The process of adding a block to the blockchain is called Bitcoin mining. When that happens, bitcoin will be rewarded for the miners. But verifying transactions by solving complex maths problem is no easy task. It takes a lot of power and energy to run these bitcoin mining computers. The PoW system ensures that the transactions in a blockchain do not duplicate and eliminates the problem of double spending.

By understanding how bitcoin and blockchain technology works, you can remove a layer of fear over this new type of investment.

For me, I knew about Bitcoin back before it took off in 2013. One of my friends introduced it to me, but I didn't understand the investment. So, when I was at the last step of creating my account with Mt Gox, a Japanese Bitcoin exchange that handled 70% of Bitcoin back in 2013, I didn't proceed to supply my verification documents because it asked me too much personal information. In short, I missed out on the bull market. I didn't have trust in this investment.

There is a saying in investing that it is important to invest in something you know about. But my takeaway lesson from Bitcoin is that it doesn't hurt to take a small risk and invest a small amount in a new type of investment. The opportunity cost of not knowing can be expensive. Risk and opportunities are two sides of the same coin. When there are risks, there are opportunities. And sometimes, you just need to go against the herd, calculate how much risk you can take, and try out new things. Sometimes, the best investments are usually those the mass is unaware.

How Blockchain works?

To invest in cryptocurrency, you need two things:

1.   Crypto wallet
2.   Exchange.

You cannot get involved into the cryptocurrency market without a crypto wallet.

A crypto wallet is a software program that manages your digital currencies. It stores your private and public keys. These keys are like the

PIN to your bank account. Your crypto wallet also has its own address called a wallet address. It mathematically relates to your private key. Think of it as a bank account number.

So, when you purchase Bitcoin from someone, that person is essentially transferring the ownership of that Bitcoin to your wallet address. For a successful transaction to happen, your private key in your crypto wallet must match the public address of the Bitcoin it is assigned to. When that happens, the detail of the transaction will be recorded in the blockchain.

There are four types of crypto wallets:

1.   Online wallet (e.g.)

2.   Mobile Wallet (e.g. http://samouraiwallet.com)

3.   Desktop Wallet (e.g. http://www.electrum.org)

4.   Hardware Wallet (e.g. http://www.bitlox.com)

5.   Paper Wallet (Print out your private and public address on paper)

Once you have a wallet, you have to find a place where cryptocurrency like Bitcoin is being exchanged. Below are some of the most popular centralized cryptocurrency exchanges:

•   Coinbase (http://www.coinbase.com)

•   Huobi (www.huobigroup.com)

•   Gemini (https://gemini.com/)

•   Coinspot (https://www.coinspot.com.au/)

•   Binance (https://www.binance.com/en)

•   Bitpanda (https://www.bitpanda.com)

•   Yobit (https://yobit.io/en/)

The main reason these sites are called centralized exchanges (CEX) is because they act just like an exchange in the stock market. They play the role as a middleman. A commission fee will be charged if you use CEX.

A decentralized cryptocurrency exchange (DEX), on the other hand, is an exchange where buyers and sellers transact without any middleman. It is pure P2P. Below is a list of the popular DEX:

- IDEX (https://idex.market/)
- StellarX (https://www.stellarx.com/)
- Bisq DEX (https://bisq.network/)

CEX and DEX both have their own pros and cons. There is no solid recommendation as to which one to use. But CEX has higher liquidity, as there are more buyers and sellers.

Whichever exchange you decide to go with, you want one with high recent trading volume. Some sites like CoinMarketCap (https://coinmarketcap.com) rank cryptocurrency exchange and cryptocurrencies by volume and liquidity. If you are invested in investing in cryptocurrency, you might want to check them out.

Top Cryptocurrency Exchanges @

CoinMarketCap ranks the top cryptocurrency exchanges based on traffic, liquidity and trading volumes.

Cryptocurrencies ▾	**Exchanges**	Watchlist					USD ▾	
Rank	Name	Web Traffic Factor @	Avg. Liquidity @	Volume (24h)	No. Markets	Change (24h)	Vol. Graph (7d)	Lat
1	◇ Binance	1000	428	$5,064,806,858	599	53.70%		J
2	↟ Huobi Global	752	418	$4,508,908,˜48	551	74.50%		Se
3	● Coinbase Pro	972	392	$425,216,˜34	65	84.16%		Ma
4	⋔ Kraken	856	382	$253,161,˜19	155	52.58%		J

Figure 13.2: Cryptocurrency Exchange

Source: CoinMarketCap

Cryptocurrency

There are thousands of cryptocurrencies existing today. It can be daunting to choose which ones to invest in. Two of the cryptocurrencies you want to look at are:

1.   Bitcoin (BTC)

2.   Ethereum (ETH)

These two cryptocurrencies have the highest market capitalization (i.e. Price x circulating supply) and are safest bet.

Although a high market cap rate is a good indicator to invest in a cryptocurrency, market capitalization doesn't tell you everything about it. There are other factors like news and upcoming events that can influence a cryptocurrency's price as well.

Like stocks, a high market cap of a cryptocurrency isn't always a good thing. Conversely, a cryptocurrency with a low cap rate might have more uprise potential.

The same logic applies to circulating supply (CS) of a cryptocurrency as well. A low CS might mean a cryptocurrency is less popular, and it might disappear one day. But a high CS might also mean it is oversupply as well.

Either way, you must do your own research when selecting a cryptocurrency to invest in. At the end of the day, the price of any cryptocurrency is governed by demand and supply. A cryptocurrency with a low supply and high demand will always have the highest potential.

[Note: Circulating Supply is the best approximate number of coins that are circulating in the market in the public.]

Top 100 Cryptocurrencies by Market Capitalization

Cryptocurrencies ▾	Exchanges	Watchlist			▽ Filters	USD ▾	Next 100 →	View All
Rank Name	Market Cap	Price	Volume (24h)	Circulating Supply	Change (24h)		Price Graph (7d)	
1 Bitcoin	$180,371,289,604	$9,802.18	$26,626,098,531	18,401,187 BTC	0.52%			
2 Ethereum	$27,354,194,465	$245.76	$10,039,550,593	111,303,883 ETH	0.62%			
3 Tether	$9,217,732,007	$1.00	$29,526,409,176	9,187,991,663 USDT *	0.16%			
4 XRP	$8,900,323,803	$0.201763	$1,144,909,290	44,112,853,111 XRP *	-0.12%			
5 Bitcoin Cash	$4,689,936,314	$254.45	$1,733,629,321	18,431,969 BCH	0.13%			
6 Bitcoin SV	$3,545,414,920	$192.37	$1,284,524,334	18,430,580 BSV	0.07%			
7 Litecoin	$3,015,133,680	$46.44	$2,181,421,692	64,930,961 LTC	1.06%			
8 Binance Coin	$2,698,825,153	$17.35	$210,588,934	155,536,713 BNB *	0.06%			

Figure 13.3: Cryptocurrency

Source: CoinMarketCap

News on Cryptocurrency

Beside doing fundamental analysis, it is important to follow cryptocurrency news if you are serious about investing or trading cryptocurrencies. Some of the most trustworthy news sites are:

1.   Coindesk (https://www.coindesk.com/)
2.   CoinMarketCal (https://coinmarketcal.com/en/)

The Bitcoin Price Roller coaster

Do you know pizza is the first product bought with bitcoins?

On 22nd May 2010, a hungry programmer purchased two large pizzas for 10,000 Bitcoins, which was worth about $30 at that time.

When Bitcoin was first launched in 2009, the price of one Bitcoin was a few dollars. It has remained a few dollars for the first few years.

Over time, Bitcoin has gained in popularity.

From 2012 to 2013, online retailers began to accept Bitcoin as a payment over the Internet. The dark web, like silk road websites, accept Bitcoin in the black market, which eventually led to its crackdown in October 2013.

In 2014, the popular Mt. Gox Bitcoin exchange, which accounts for 70% of all Bitcoin transactions, traded around 150,000 Bitcoins per day, also got shutdown because it was accused of fraud.

At the infancy stage of Bitcoin, there was a lot of scepticism about it indeed.

It is not until 2013 when Bitcoin's price really started to rise. At the beginning of 2013, Bitcoin was trading at $13.5 USD. By early April, it hit $220 USD, and then pulled back to $70 USD in mid-April. Then in October, Bitcoin was trading at $100 USD. By November's end, it surged to $1,075 USD. Bitcoin suddenly took off because it attracted

Bitcoin miners from China to enter the marketplace. This is exactly what happened if you look at the tiny rally in the chart.

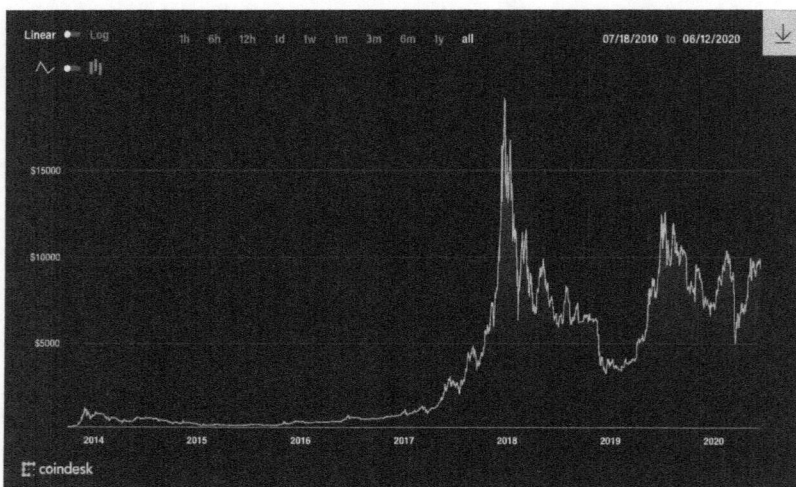

Figure 13.4: Bitcoin Price
Source: CoinMarketCap

Bitcoin became very volatile after it reached its new high. The collapse of the Mt. Gox exchange caused Bitcoin to fall further. Bitcoin was trading at only about $315 USD at the beginning of 2015, but by 2016, Bitcoin was rising steadily again. In early 2017, it broke $1,000 USD.

The real rally in Bitcoin didn't happen until 2017. In October 2017, Bitcoin hit $5,000 USD. One month later, in November 2017, it doubled to $10,000 USD. By December 2017, it hit $20,000 USD. In a matter of months, it crashed back down to $7,000 USD. By April 2018, it had plunged below $3,500 USD.

Back in 2018, many commentators compared the rollercoaster rise of Bitcoin price to the dotcom bubble or the tulip mania.

However, as more and more countries like China, Australia, and big financial institutions like J.P. Morgan also invested in cryptocurrency, the role of Bitcoin and the cryptocurrency market overall is just going to gain more and more confidence in the future.

Chapter 14

Hidden Secrets of Commodity

Commodity is rarely under the radar screen of investors. It is one of the least respected asset classes. While commodity might not be a definite path to true wealth for most people, it is more for speculators or traders. The reason I include commodity investing in this chapter is for readers to understand more about different asset classes in the world of investing.

To me, it just doesn't make sense to ignore the whole asset class completely.

When you are investing in commodity, you are investing in raw materials, natural resources and hard assets – things you can touch and see. When you enter the supermarket or grocery stores, you are surrounded by many different commodities – rice, coffee, sugar and oil, etc. Do you sometimes wonder why the price of these daily commodities does not fluctuate much like stock?

It is because the futures market of commodity makes the price stable.

How the Future Market Works?

Imagine a farmer, Mary, has planted 30,000 bushels of corns in September when the price was $3.5 per bushel. However, she will only be able to harvest and sell in December. By December, Mary is most likely to receive a different price. If the price rises, Mary will have more earnings. On the other hand, if the price drops, Mary will have less profit.

Meanwhile, Marco, the boss of a cereal company, is also trying to fix the buy price for corn so that he can forecast his earnings and future production.

This is where the futures market fits in.

Fortunately, corn can be stored. Mary and Marco can hedge against the price change by entering a futures contract. A futures contract is a legal agreement to buy or sell a particular commodity asset at a predetermined price at a specified time in the future.

Future Contract

Delivery Date:
28th December 2020

Quantity
5000 Bushels

Quantity
$3.5

Signature _____

Figure 14.1: Future Contract

Source: Author

By entering a futures contract like the example above, Mary has the obligation to deliver 5,000 bushels of corns at $3.5 per bushel by 28th

December 2020. Marco, on the other hand, has the obligation to buy and receive 5,000 bushels of corns when the futures contract expires.

Under a futures contract, both Mary and Marco do not need to worry about a change in price. Mary can lock in a certain harvest price for her corn to avoid a drop in price in the future. In other words, she does not need to worry about the price volatility, as the price is transferred from the producer to the speculators who bought the futures contract.

Let's say in December, the price falls to $2.5 per bushel. If Mary did not enter a futures contract, she will lose $1 per bushel. Conversely, if she did, she will hedge against the loss. By entering a futures contract, she is going to sell at $3.5 per bushel regardless of how high or low the spot price of a bushel of corn is.

Another thing is that for a loss of $1 per bushel in the cash market, there is always going to be a $1 gain per bushel in the futures market. If you are losing in a futures contract, buying the commodity in the cash market can help to offset your futures position.

	Cash Market	Future Market
September	Price of corn is $3.5 per bushel	Sell Corn future at $3.5 per bushel
December	Sell corn at $2.5 per bushel	Buy Corn future at $2.5 per bushel
Change	Loss of $1 per bushel	Profit of $1 per bushel

Table 14.1: Future contract can hedge against loss

Source: Author

Although the futures market protects producers and hedges against their risk, they need to be volatile and attractive enough for speculators and investors to jump in and buy these futures contracts. Sometimes, the speculation on the commodity market causes an artificial demand on the commodity, which leads to a higher price on the physical commodity.

[Note: The concept of futures trading today has a humble origin. The Dojima Rice Exchange was the world's first commodity futures exchange. It was established in 1697 in Osaka, Japan, by samurai who sought to control the rice markets.]

Why Should You Invest in Commodity?

Commodities have a low to negative correlation with a traditional asset class like stock. When commodities are in a bear market, companies in the manufacturing sectors tends to do well.

Barry Bannister and Paul Forward created an analysis between the equity market and the commodity market in the U.S. from 1870 to today. Their finding is that approximately every 18 years, the stock market and the commodity change cycles. If you examine the diagram below, the stock market beats the commodity from 1980 to 2000, and then in the next 18 years, the commodity market beats back the stock market.

One theory I can think of is because when the commodity price is down, companies can purchase raw material inexpensively. They can produce things that people want to buy at a cheaper price, and thus higher earning. So, that is why stocks in general will do well.

Figure 14.2: U.S. Stock Market relative to commodity market

Source: war, legacy and social cost

[Note: For listed companies that produce commodity, they tend to do well in a bull market is commodity.]

A Brief Introduction to Commodity Exchange

The CME Group is the largest futures exchange in the world. It consists of the Chicago Mercantile Exchange (CME), the Chicago Board of Trade (CBOT), New York Mercantile Exchange (NYMEX), Commodity Exchange Inc. (COMEX), the Kansas City Board of Trade (KCBT), and the NEX Group, which were previously independent exchanges. The CME Group was created in 2007 when CME merged with CBOT. The CME Group provides the largest range of products in the futures market you can imagine.

The Intercontinental Exchange (ICE) is another exchange in U.S. future trading. It was founded in 2000 and began as an electronic energy-trading platform. With the acquisition of the New York Board of Trade (NYBOT) in 2007, it is now the CME Group's largest competitor.

And. of course, U.S. is not the only country that has futures exchange. Some of the largest futures exchange outside the U.S. includes the Shanghai Future Exchange in China, the National Stock Exchange of India, Eurex in Europe, the Moscow Exchange in Russia, and Korea Exchange.

The Six Commodity Sectors

Commodity can be divided into six different sectors. Each sector has their own unique cycles and different returns.

1.   Industrial Metals (e.g., Aluminum, Copper, Nickel, Zinc, Tin, Lead)

2.   Energy (e.g., Crude Oil, Gasoline, Natural Gas)

3.   Precious Metals (e.g., Platinum, Palladium, Silver, Gold)

4.   Grains (e.g., corn, soybean oil, soybean, wheat)

5.   Softs (e.g., cocoa, coffee, sugar, cotton)

6.   Livestock (e.g., live cattle)

For example, right now, the world is contending with the coronavirus epidemic. It has largely impacted sectors, such as energy and soft metals. In fact, on 21st April 2020, U.S. oil prices plunged into negative territory, which is unprecedented in history. Anyone who sells a barrel of oil would have to pay the buyer because of how oil was traded. Futures contracts required buyers to take possession of oil, but nobody wanted the oil because there was no place to store it.

But not all commodities were hit hard during this unprecedented time.

Adverse weather contributed to an increase in rice price despite most other agricultural commodity price falling.

That is why it is important to do a fundamental analysis of the commodity to know what affects a particular commodity in a sector.

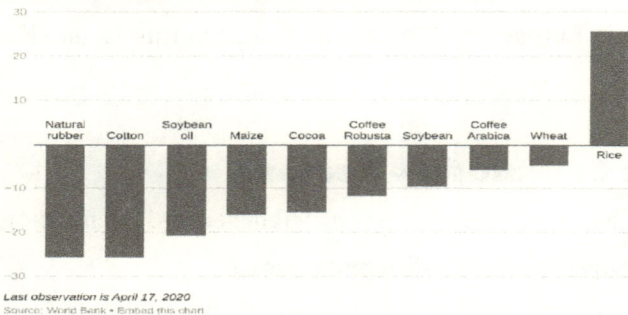

Adverse weather contributed to an increase in rice prices, but most other agricultural commodity prices fell

Percent change in commodity prices from the week of January 13-17 to April 13-17

Last observation is April 17, 2020
Source: World Bank • Embed this chart

Figure 14.3: Percentage change in commodity price

Source: World Bank

How to Invest in Commodity?

There are four different ways to invest in commodities:

1. Investing directly in the commodity.

2. Using commodity futures contracts to invest.

3. Buying shares of exchange-traded funds that specialize in commodities.

4. Buying shares of stock in companies that produce commodities.

This chapter will focus on commodity futures contracts. It is the most profitable way to invest in commodity because of leverage. But it is also the number one way to lose money.

But where do you find these futures contracts?

If you Google *futures quote*, you will come up with a list of sites like barchart.com. Inside, you can find the future price of commodities. Take grain as an example. If you examine each row, you will find that each contract will have a symbol, contract name, and the price information.

Grains Futures Prices   Fri, Jun 12th, 2020   Help ⑦

Receive End-of-Day Email (Grains)

FULL LIST   CURRENCIES   ENERGIES   FINANCIALS   GRAINS   INDICES   MEATS   METALS   SOFTS

Intraday   ⌄   Main View   ⌄   ⚡ flipcharts   ⬇ download
Latest futures price quotes as of Fri, Jun 12th, 2020.

Grains

Symbol	Contract Name	Last	Change	Open	High	Low	Volume	Time	Links
+ ZCN20	Corn (Jul '20)	330-0s	+0-2	329-4	333-0	328-2	219,907	06/12/20	⋮
+ ZCU20	Corn (Sep '20)	334-4s	-0-4	334-4	337-6	333-4	149,424	06/12/20	⋮
+ ZCZ20	Corn (Dec '20)	343-0s	-0-6	343-2	345-6	341-6	77,844	06/12/20	⋮
+ ZSN20	Soybean (Jul '20)	871-2s	+5-2	866-4	873-0	863-4	123,832	06/12/20	⋮
+ ZSQ20	Soybean (Aug '20)	872-4s	+4-4	868-4	875-2	866-0	32,404	06/12/20	⋮
+ ZSX20	Soybean (Nov '20)	879-6s	+3-0	876-6	884-4	874-4	75,956	06/12/20	⋮
+ ZMN20	Soybean Meal (Jul '20)	289.0s	-0.7	289.6	292.8	288.5	47,520	06/12/20	⋮
+ ZMQ20	Soybean Meal (Aug '20)	291.4s	-0.8	292.1	295.0	291.1	10,729	06/12/20	⋮
+ ZMZ20	Soybean Meal (Dec '20)	298.4s	-1.1	299.0	301.9	298.3	25,525	06/12/20	⋮
+ ZLN20	Soybean Oil (Jul '20)	27.50s	unch	27.50	27.78	27.30	58,677	06/12/20	⋮
+ ZLQ20	Soybean Oil (Aug '20)	27.70s	+0.01	27.77	27.97	27.50	22,289	06/12/20	⋮

Figure 14.4: Grains Future Price

Source: barchart.com

In the first row, we have ZCN20, which is a contact for Corn (Jul '20). The symbol tells you a lot of information about what the contract is about. The first two letters 'ZC' means the contract ticker symbol for corn. For crude oil, the ticker symbol is "CL." For gold, the ticker symbol is 'GC.' If you Google *futures ticker symbols*, you can find a lot of contract tickers in both the commodity market and the financial market. The third letter 'N' in ZCN20 refers to the month the contract expires, which is July. And '20" is the year the contract expires. So, ZCN20 basically refers to a corn futures contracts that is going to expire on July 2020.

Month	Code
January	F
February	G
March	H
April	J
May	K
June	M
July	N
August	Q
September	U
October	V
November	X
December	Z

Table 14.2: Month Quote

Source: Author

If you click inside and look at the ZCN20 specification, the first thing you will notice is 330-0s. This is not a price in currency as there is no dollar sign next to it. It might surprise you that futures are not priced in currency, but in points.

The unit of measurement for a point in the futures market is a tick. Each tick has a distance and a worth. Ticks are different for different commodities, depending on the type of futures contract. A tick of one commodity like corn is not the same as the tick for gold. For example, corn has a tick of ¼ cent per bushel. Since a contract for ZC has 5,000 bushels, each tick movement in this contract is $12.5. (1/4 cents x $5000 = 1250 cents or $12.5) Say, if ZCN20 is up by two ticks today, it means that the price of the ZCN20 contract rose by $25. However, this way of calculating profit is difficult. That is why we use a multiplier in futures contracts. In ZCN20, the multiplier is 50, meaning the value of 1 futures unit is $50. Let's say corn is trading $3/bushel and moves up 1 cent to $3.01/bushel. That 1 cent needs to be multiplied by 5,000 bushels in a futures contract, which equals $50. So, if you heard the financial news, saying corn is up by 7 cents for the day, you will know the move in the futures contract is 7 x $50 = $350.

Corn Jul '20 (ZCN20)
330-0s +0-2 (**+0.08%**) 06/12/20 [CBOT]
CONTRACT SPECIFICATIONS for Fri, Jun 12th, 2020   Alerts 🔔   Watch ⭐   Help ⑦

Barchart Symbol	ZC
Exchange Symbol	ZC
Contract	Corn
Exchange	CBOT
Tick Size	1/4 cent per bushel ($12.50 per contract)
Daily Limit	25 cents per bushel ($1,250 per contract) Expanded limit 40 cents
Contract Size	5,000 bushels
Trading Months	Mar, May, Jul, Sep, Dec (H, K, N, U, Z)
Trading Hours	7:00p.m. - 7:45a.m. and 8:30a.m. - 1:20p.m. (Settles 1:15p.m.) (Sun-Fri) CST
Value of One Futures Unit	$50
Value of One Options Unit	$50
Last Trading Day	The business day prior to the 15th calendar day of the contract month

Figure 14.5: ZCN20

Source: barchart.com

Commodity quotes refrain from showing the denominator of the fraction because it is always assumed to be 8. So, if you see ZCN20 display on the board as 330-2, 2 is the reduced fraction of 2/8. Once you know this, you will realize a quarter of a cent is denoted by -2 or 2/8, half a cent is denoted by -4 or 4/8, and three quarters of a cent is denoted by -6 or 6/8.

2/8 or -2	0.25 cents
4/8 or -4	0.50 cents
6/8 or -6	0.75 cents

If you bought ZCN20 when it opens at 329-4, it means ZCN20 opens at 329 points and 0.5 cents (2 ticks). And if it sells at 330-0, it means you profited 2 ticks, which is $25. (1 tick is $12.5).

Before you buy a futures contract, you need to find a broker and open an account with them. Google *low account minimum futures broker*, and you will be able to find a long list of them. Some of these futures brokers only require you to deposit a minimum of $500 to open an account and start trading. The reason to find a broker for commodity trading is because they will give you leverage with margin. They connect you with buyers and sellers. And you will need to pay a commission fee for both buying and selling of a contract.

So, when you enter a futures contract of ZCN20, it has a contract size of 5,000 bushels, with each bushel costing $3.30 USD. So, the total cost of ZCN20 futures contracts is 16,500 USD. However, investing in commodity allows you to use margin. It means you do not need to put down $16,500, and you only need to put down the initial margin requirements, which costs 25% of the contract. However, when using margin in futures trading, the margin maintenance requires you to return the margin to the initial margin level in case loss on a future position happens.

[Note: Initial margin requirement is the amount of capital an exchange expects a trader to have as deposit in his or her account to buy, sell or hold a single contract. Maintenance margin is the minimum account balance that must be maintained to avoid a margin call. Maintenance margin is normally 90% of the initial margin.]

Say, you fulfil the initial margin requirements to enter futures contract ZCN20 by putting down $5,000. And the maintenance margin is $4,500. Let's say if the price of corn goes up from $3.30 to $3.50 (i.e., 6% increase), you are up $0.2 per bushel in corn, or $1,000 ($0.2 x 5,000) profit (i.e., ROI = 20%). However, if the price of corn drops from $3.30 to $3.10 (i.e., 6% increase), you are down $0.2 per bushel in corn, or

$1,000 ($0.2 x 5,000) loss (i.e., ROI = - 20%). When this happens, your account balance will be $4,000, which is below the maintenance margin requirement. An additional $1,000 must be put back to bring the account balance back to the initial margin level.

Once you have decided to invest in commodity, remember to use the same technique as you invest in stock. You must always do fundamental analysis and technical analysis, position yourself with options and hedge your risks with orders. Always use stop orders when you are investing in the commodity market. More importantly, always have a plan and go with the trend.

Hidden Secrets of Commodity

I hope by now that you have a basic understanding of how to invest in commodity using futures contracts. The reason why I think everyone should pay attention to the commodity market is because commodity is very, very undervalued right now in 2020.

Since governments around the world are printing currency like crazy, the fluctuating value of the dollar makes it very hard to gauge whether value of commodity are actually rising or falling. In here, we are going to look at the commodity price in ounces of gold. By dividing a commodity in gold, once again, we are essentially removing the dollar from the equation and measuring its true value.

Below is a chart on the WTI Crude oil price measured in gold gram per barrel from 1990 till 2020. As you can see, the price barrel of WTI crude oil in gold is volatile. It fluctuates between 0.5 grams of gold to 4 grams of gold.

Right now, oil is very, very undervalued compared to its historic average.

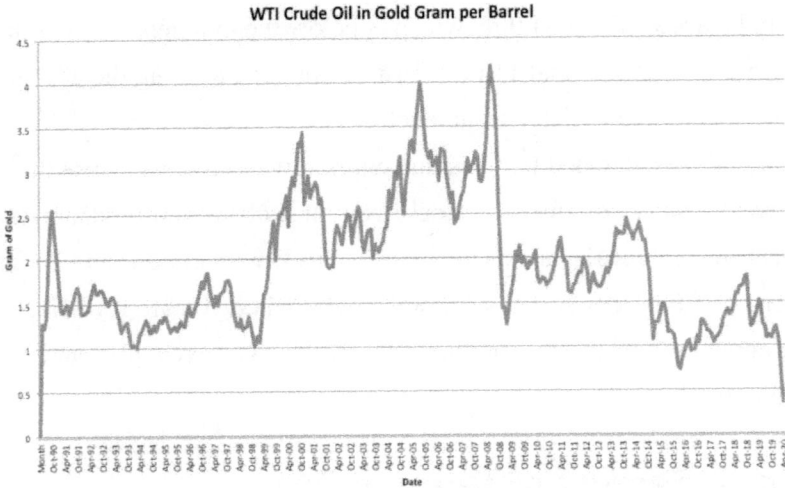

Figure 14.6 WTI Crude Oil in Gold Gram per barrel

Source: Author

It is not only oil that has crashed against gold. Many commodities measured in gold have crashed. The reason why everything seems to be so expensive today is because the value of our dollar is decreasing rapidly. If you are saving in gold instead of the dollar, you will experience deflation, not inflation. That is why I encourage you as an investor to start seeing things in value, not in price. By doing so, you will be able to spot rare opportunities that only a few investors can find.

Chapter 15

Hidden Secrets of FOREX

Every day, trillions of dollars are traded on the foreign exchange market. The foreign exchange (also known as FX or FOREX) market is a global marketplace for exchanging national currencies against one another. It is the most liquid financial market in the world. But it is also one of the least understood markets.

Foreign Exchange Reserve

Foreign reserves (FX reserves) are currencies of other countries held by central banks around the world. Central banks buy currencies of other countries to suppress the value of their own currency to boost trade competitiveness. Trade surplus countries want a weak currency to boost export, which results in more employment and economic growth.

Central banks acquire FX reserve by printing their own local currency. They use the newly-created currency to purchase the currency from other country.

For example, when China trades with the U.S., Chinese businessmen ship products to the U.S., the dollars coming into China were bought back by the People's Bank of China (PBOC) to exchange back to RMB before entering the Chinese economy. PBOC does that by printing RMB to buy the dollar at a fixed exchange rate. These dollars were held as FX reserves. This tactic is very beneficial to China's export led growth economy.

As of Q4 2019, the world's total foreign exchange reserve is $11.8 trillion. 60.89% of the allocated reserves were held in U.S dollars as equity, debt instruments like the U.S. government debt or direct foreign investment into the U.S.

World (US Dollars, Billions)

	Q4 2018	Q1 2019	Q2 2019	Q3 2019	Q4 2019
˅ Total Foreign Exchange Reserves	11,435.90	11,610.61	11,737.60	11,658.48	11,829.54
˅ Allocated Reserves	10,727.03	10,897.83	11,021.03	10,927.43	11,078.43
Claims in U.S. dollars	6,623.30	6,727.09	6,751.43	6,725.88	6,745.65
Claims in euro	2,217.38	2,208.79	2,264.88	2,210.82	2,275.95
Claims in Chinese renminbi	203.08	211.92	212.44	215.82	217.67
Claims in Japanese yen	557.65	584.63	611.87	613.89	631.44
Claims in pounds sterling	474.17	495.70	497.41	492.14	511.81
Claims in Australian dollars	173.95	181.95	186.71	182.58	187.31
Claims in Canadian dollars	197.22	208.64	209.85	205.40	207.98
Claims in Swiss francs	15.29	15.27	15.53	15.93	16.98
Claims in other currencies	264.99	263.84	270.92	264.97	283.64

Figure 15.1: Total Foreign Exchange Reserve

Source: IMF

If you study monetary history, you will discover that the majority of the world's foreign exchange reserves come from the U.S. running huge trade deficit with the rest of the world. As central banks of trade surplus countries print their own currency by buying the dollar enters into their economy, they reinvest it into buying U.S. dollar denominated assets like the U.S. Treasury Bond. This way, these trade surplus countries help the U.S. to boost its economy and the U.S., in return, can continue to buy more goods inexpensively from these trade surplus countries.

In fact, some trade surplus countries are holding a lot in foreign reserves. China, for example, is holding $3.1 trillion USD as foreign reserves. This accounts for 61% of China's total assets in Q2 2020.

When foreign central banks buys dollar denominated assets like the U.S. Treasury Bond, it pushes up the price of the Bond and drives the yield down. This causes the Federal Reserve to lose control of the U.S. interest rate, which stays at zero today.

[Note: PBOC's total asset is 36,034.76 billion RMB as of Q2 2020, which is $5.08 trillion USD]

What Drives Currencies Today?

When looking at the movement of currencies, we categorise it into long time outlook and short time outlook.

In the long-term, the direction on currencies movement is dictated by trade imbalances.

Countries with current account surpluses have more room to experience currency appreciation. Countries with current account deficit will be more likely to experience currency depreciation. Below is a chart showing the current account of Japan, China, U.S. and U.K.

If you look at China and Japan, they have a currency account surplus. Their currencies are too weak and have more room to appreciate in the long run.

U.S. and U.K., on the other hand, have a trade deficit. Their currencies are more likely to depreciate in the long run.

Figure 15.2: Current Account Balance of Four Countries

Source: World Bank

How about the exchange rate in the short-term outlook?

In the short-term, fundamentally, it used to be the interest rate differentials between countries that decided the exchange rate. For example, if you plot a graph of the U.S. 10 year yield vs. the Japanese 10-year government bond yield, and compare it with the USD/JPY, you will discover a relationship between the currency pair (USD/JPY) and the USD-JPY rate differential.

Figure 15.3:Interest Rate Differentials of 10 Year US Treasury Yield and 10 Year Japan

Treasury Yield

Source: Stockchart.com

However, as I am writing now in 2020, most countries already had their interest rate driven close to zero. The new factor that drives currency is overtaken by the scale of fiat currency creation, which depends on the size of the Quantitative easing (QE).

By anticipating what the central bank will do next in their monetary policy, you may able to guess the movement of currencies. Whenever the U.S. launches a new round of QE, other countries must launch their own version of QE in order to keep the exchange rate stable. By comparing the total asset in the balance sheet of one country with another, you can project where the short-term interest rate might be going today.

Let me give you an example. The USD/AUD has risen sharply from 1.4 at the beginning of Jan 2020 to a high of 1.7 by March 2020. Due to the COVID-19 epidemic, in mid-March, 2020, the Federal Reserve returned to QE by injecting $1.4 trillion into the economy by repurchasing short-term lending agreements, and slashed its interest rate to zero. In Australia, we also cut the interest rate down from 0.5 to 0.25. When that happens, we see a plunge in USD/AUD.

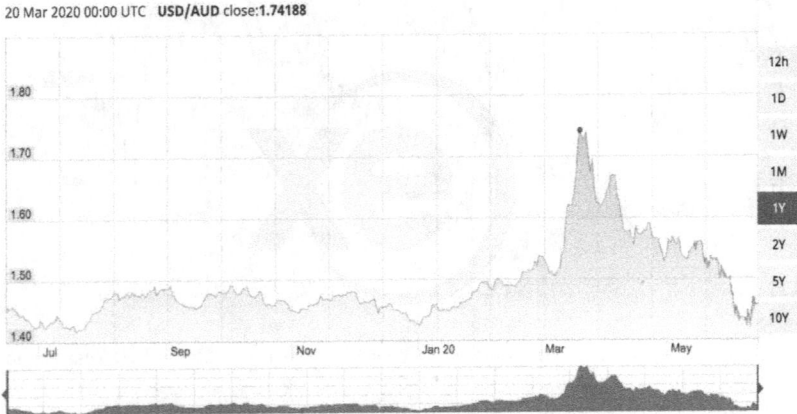

Figure 15.4: USD/AUD

Source: XE Currency

The truth is that it is not just the Federal Reserve in the U.S that is launching QE. In fact, all the central banks around the world are racing to debase their currency and expand their balance sheet dramatically. In March 2020, the Bank of England announced a fresh £200 billion and slashed their interest rate down to 0.1%. About the same time, ECB, an analogy for the Federal Reserve of Europe, announced that it would buy an additional €750 billion in its asset purchase program until the epidemic is over. In April 2020, the PBOC also injected 56 billion RMB into the Chinese economy.

The size of these QE packages and the conditions of QE is going to play a major role in deciding the short-term interest rate in the post COVID-19 economy.

Chapter 16

Final Words

Finally, I would like to thank you for taking the time to read this book. It is a long journey.

I hope I have exposed you to the hidden secrets of investing across most asset classes. More importantly, I hope you enjoy reading it.

Before closing this book, I wish to share my thoughts with you on charting an investing plan. In my experience, if you are starting off in investing in your 20s or 30s, it is very important that you invest in real estate first before investing in other asset classes. By doing so, you are giving yourself a lot of unfair advantages because of leverage through debt. In the 21st century, debt is the new money. When you invest in real estate, you are positioning yourself to reap the benefit from inflation and taxation. Best of all, you are creating wealth for yourself. Your primary investment goal should be to accumulate as much cashflow real estate as possible so that you can become financially independent.

Second, depending on your age, I strongly encourage you to put aside a percentage of your entire portfolio and save it in gold and silver. Learn to see the value of a commodity, not its price in dollars. Last but not least, have your own money rules and follow them religiously. Remember that if you do not have money rules, money will rule you.

I believe your dedication to achieve your investing goals is the currency of your success.

I wish you all the best in your investing journey.

Happy Investing.

Recommended Readings
To further enhance your financial diligent

Investing

The Intelligent Investor (**Benjamin Graham**)

Guide to Investing in Gold and Silver (**Michael Maloney**)

The Art of the Deal (**Donald J. Trump**)

Trump Never Give Up (**Donald J. Trump**)

The Snowball: Warren Buffett and the Business of Life (**Alice Schroder**)

Cashflow Quadrant (**Robert T. Kiyosaki**)

Irrational Exuberance (**Robert J. Shiller**)

Extraordinary Delusions and the Madness of Crowds (**Charles Mackay**)

Monetary History and Money

Gold (**Nathan Lewis**)

The Dollar Crisis (**Richard Duncan**)

A Primer on Money, Banking and Gold (**Peter L. Bernstein**)

A Monetary History of the United States, 1857-1960 (**Milton Friedman**)

About the Author

Marco Chu Kwan Ching
Author, Investor

I began my profession as an electrical engineer in TOSHIBA after graduating from *The University of New South Wales* (UNSW) in 2009. I had a small web design business for indexing restaurants. I was firmly sitting on the dream of most undergraduates- a job and a part time business. With the collapse of the global economy in 2008, I first noticed how the effects of the financial crisis unfolded. I experienced the accelerating inflation rapidly eroding our wealth. I witnessed the foreclosures of businesses, income polarization, the interventions of the Government monetary policies. Even with little life experience on these subjects, I know something is not right. The current financial system is developing cracks. This sparked my interest in studying monetary history and the global economy. I set out to research the answers myself.

What I found shocked me to my core. The root of all the problems lie within our philosophy of money. The definition of money is flawed. Currency is not money. The original idea of money being a container to store the value of our labor, time, ideas, and talents are replaced by debts. Money, rather than being a store of value, becomes a plan to transfer our wealth away from us. My mission is to educate as many people as possible about these findings, so they are armed with the right knowledge to protect themselves and their family from this corrupt monetary system. That's why I am willing to give up my time to work on the material that now appears in the *Corruption of Real Money Series*.

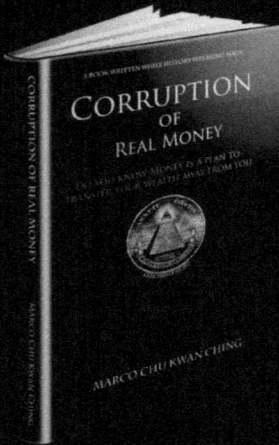

Thank you for Reading!

Thank you for reading this book! I know you could have picked from a dozens of books about this subject, but you took a chance with mine and I appreciate it.

Lastly, I just have one small request,

If you believe that this book is worth sharing, would you take a few seconds to let your friends know about it too? If you love my work, please feel free to leave a positive feedback on Amazon and Goodreads.

My contact:
https://www.facebook.com/marco.chu.10
https://www.goodreads.com/author/show/15944678.Marco_Chu_
Kwan_Ching

Corruption of Real Money Facebook Page
https://www.facebook.com/CorruptionOfRealMoney/

Corruption of Real Money Twitter Page
https://twitter.com/CorruptionofMor_

Goodreads Page
https://www.goodreads.com/book/show/54391982-hidden-secrets-of-
investing

Corruption of Real Money Website
http://www.corruptionofrealmoney.com

***

Book Series by Marco Chu Kwan Ching

1 Corruption of Real Money (Monetary History and Global Economy)
  http://www.corruptionofrealmoney.com

2 Terrorlands (Children's Horror Fiction)
  http://www.terrorlands.com/

www.ingramcontent.com/pod-product-compliance
Lightning Source LLC
Chambersburg PA
CBHW031844200326
41597CB00012B/262